hostas

and other shade-loving plants

hostas
and other shade-loving plants

Richard Bird with David Tarrant

WHITECAP BOOKS
Vancouver/Toronto

5131

Hostas and other shade-loving plants
This edition published in 1999 by
Whitecap Books Ltd., 351 Lynn Avenue
North Vancouver, B.C., Canada V7J 2C4

© 1999 Quadrillion Publishing Limited,
Woolsack Way, Godalming, Surrey,
GU7 1XW, UK.

Canadian Cataloguing in Publication Data

Bird, Richard

   Hostas and other shade-loving plants

     Includes index.

     ISBN 1-55110-823-2

     1. Hosta. 2. Shade-tolerant plants.

     3. Gardening in the shade.

    I. Tarrant, David. II. Title.

SB434.7.B57 1999   653.9'543

C98-911107-5

Printed in Italy

ISBN 1-55110-823-2

Jacket: Hostas and
*Euphorbia amygdaloides
robbiae* in a shady border.

page 1: Shade-loving
Pulmonaria saccharata.

page 2: Hosta leaves after
a rain shower.

page 4: The filigree fronds
of the ostrich fern,
Matteuccia struthiopteris.

All text by Richard Bird, except the following
sections, by David Tarrant:
p18 Problem Areas; p31 Instant Leafmold;
p36 Shade for Cold Climates; p50 Planting
Under Trees; p68 Glorious Trumpets; p83 A
Scheme for all Seasons; p86 Success in Dry
Soil; p95 A Slugproof Hosta

Credits

Editor: Joanna Smith
Designer: Mark Buckingham
Design Manager: Justina Leitão
Project Editor: Jane Alexander

Artworks: Vana Haggerty
Indexer: Hilary Bird
Americanizer: Catriona Tudor Erler
Production: Sandra Dixon, Janine Seddon
Production Director: Graeme Proctor

contents

foreword

If you have sometimes despaired of gardening in the shade, this is the book for you. It will open your eyes to a whole new world of luscious foliage, plant textures and subtle nuances of color. Here at last is a book that shows it is possible to have a garden – and a beautiful garden – in the shade.

Having gardened in a very shady townhouse courtyard some years ago, and now on a north-facing roof garden, I have experimented with quite a few plants and have always found it a challenge. (This, I might add, promotes the love of gardening in all of us.) Working at a botanical garden, I have always found plenty of inspirational ideas to duplicate on a smaller scale at home, but there was never very much

written about shade gardening to help. Now shade gardening is a concept that's really coming into its own, especially with the growing awareness of ecological concerns.

Along with the environmental movement comes the understanding that well-planted shade areas allow refuge for interesting birds and happy slug-eating toads, among other welcome garden creatures. There also seems to be a better understanding of the use of native vegetation, and happily many nurseries are now beginning to propagate these plants for the industry. Most gardeners have a voracious appetite for new and different exotic

plants, however, and the plant lists in this book will not disappoint them.

The plant lists are well researched, easy to follow and should encourage readers to be adventuresome when it comes to the challenging shady areas of the garden. The book deals with every shaded garden scenario and possibly has the best directory yet of shade-loving plants for temperate to cooler regions of the world. I feel sure that after reading this book, you will fill those dark corners with the golden or blue foliage of hostas, the chartreuse flowers of lady's mantle or the soft green of ferns, so that when friends come to visit they will be in awe of your creativity.

—David Tarrant

Far left: Persicaria bistorta 'Superba', *Hosta* 'Gold Standard', hellebores and ferns surround a large pot in a shady border.

Shady areas are often considered a problem in gardens. In fact they rarely are; the myth has only come about because many gardeners have tried to grow sun-loving plants there. These, naturally, have found the shade far from their liking and have either languished and become leggy and very much out of character, or they have rapidly turned up their toes and died. Likewise many have not liked the dry conditions and have quickly become unhealthy and succumbed to all manner of diseases including mildew.

On the other hand there is another breed of gardeners who positively love the shade, and even go so far as deliberately to create it. These gardeners are the ones who work with nature, rather than attempting to fight it. Instead of planting sun-loving plants in the shade, they choose those that grow in shade in the wild; those that have adapted themselves to the conditions of little direct sunlight and the possibility of low water availability.

As well as choosing the right plants they also adapt the shade so that it is more to the liking of the plants they want to grow; they may prune overhead trees to allow in more light or modify the soil so that it becomes more like a moist woodland soil. In

introduction

Plants are great opportunists and have made it their business to colonize almost every corner of the world, even the most inhospitable. To many plants, shade is inhospitable, but others have seized the opportunity to fill the spaces below trees and shrubs.

this book we hope to take the reader through the various stages of creating a shade garden. It starts by looking at the shady conditions that plants experience in the wild and how they cope with them. There is nothing complicated about it and it all seems quite obvious when it has been explained. It then goes on to see how conditions

like these can be provided in the garden; again, nothing complicated, just good gardening practice.

Once the scene has been set it is time to consider the plants themselves. One might get the impression that shade-loving plants are rather a dull lot, but this is far from the truth. Although there are a few with bright colors, impatiens for example, it has to be admitted that color is not always as vivid as in the open sun, but within shady conditions this is not important. Often in the shade it is the pale colors that produce a far more dramatic effect. Foliage also plays an important role. The great range of different greens can create a wonderfully restful but interesting scene. On the other hand the variegations, especially in plants such as hostas, can add sudden dramatic splashes of light and interest. The different shapes and textures of foliage are also important. The filigree effects of ferns contrast well with the more solid shape of plants such as hostas. On the other hand many of the shiny leaves, hollies for example, reflect light and illuminate shady areas.

Although the spring is undoubtedly the best time of year for the shade garden, mainly because the shade is not too dense then, there is plenty

Far left: As well as providing a suitable environment for many plants, shady areas are often also the most comfortable for humans.

Above: Hardy geraniums, such as this *Geranium sanguineum striatum*, are among the most beautiful and versatile of shade-loving plants.

Right: The leaves of *Alchemilla mollis* are at their most handsome after a rain shower.

Far right: Hosta fortunei albopicta, a yellow *Trollius* and the soft golden grass, *Milium effusum* 'Aureum', create a sunny scene in a shady spot.

happening all the year round, even during the winter when you would expect there to be nothing.

It is not only plants that enjoy shade, it also plays a very important part in the outdoor life of people. Eating and entertaining in the shade is often far more pleasant than being out in the naked sun. In very hot weather, deep, cool shade is often appreciated but for most uses, a light dappled shade with the sunlight just playing through the leaves is ideal. Shade also has the merit of forming an enclosed space, and thus giving a sense of secu-

rity, and yet at the same time being open to the elements; an ideal combination for relaxation.

The message, then, of this book is not to be frightened of the shady parts of the garden. Rather than abandoning them, go out and embrace them, turning them into some of the most enjoyable areas of the garden. There are so many plants that will grow in shade, there must surely be something that fits in with your style of gardening, and if there isn't then it is worth experimenting and extending your experience and expertise.

When choosing plants to grow in a shady part of the garden, far better results will be obtained by working with nature rather than fighting against it. In other words, it makes much more sense to grow plants that would naturally grow in shade, and would therefore be used to such conditions, than to attempt to grow sun-loving plants which would undoubtedly languish and soon die out in a shady spot. In order to get the best out of one's plants it is, therefore, essential to understand how they live in the wild and how we can possibly adapt these conditions to our gardens at home. The first thing we need to consider is light levels.

Nearly all plants need light so that photosynthesis can take place. Their leaves absorb the light and through various chemical processes, foods are produced which help to maintain the health and vigor of the plant. Some plants have, however, become adapted so that they can live in less than ideal situations, that is places where there is less light. A few have modified themselves so much that they no longer need to photosynthesize at all, as they have become parasitic and live off other plants. A few of these, such as the bird's nest orchid, *Neottia nidus-avis*, will grow in dense shade, under beech trees for

light and shade

By understanding the way light and shade can affect a garden, the gardener can work with nature rather than trying to struggle against it. It makes all the difference if you choose the right plants for the right place.

example, where little else can be persuaded to grow well.

However, for practical gardening purposes, it is safe to say that most plants need plenty of light and do best out in the open, while a still considerable number are happy to grow in varying degrees of shade. In the wild most of this shade is produced by

other plants, particularly in the form of woodlands and forests in the more temperate regions and tropical jungles around the equator. Having said that, it is quite possible for shady conditions to be produced by a single tree or bush, which is of great importance to the gardener who is unlikely to have a forest or jungle on his or her doorstep.

There are many plants that will grow either in shade or in the open, as long as the former is not too dense. Hostas are good examples of these. However, it is not just a question of planting them either in the open or shade, rather more care is needed than that. Nearly all shade-loving plants that can be grown in the open need to have a damp position, or at least they need to be grown in a soil that contains a lot of good moisture-retentive material. On the other hand, some plants that prefer to be grown in sun can be induced to grow in light shade by trimming back tree or shrub branches above so that more light filters through.

In order to understand fully the plants we intend to grow it is necessary to look a bit more closely at the woodland structure. Woods and forests are the natural climax, the end result of letting nature take over a bit of ground. If we look at a piece of

Far left: Sugar maples, *Acer saccharum*, provide light shade and stunning fall color.

Above: A shady patio in a garden surrounded by trees. This sloping bed shows the wide range of interesting shrubs and ground cover plants that can be grown in shade. Azaleas steal the show in late spring.

Right: Bracken (*Pteridium aquilinum*) colonizes a glade in a woodland, making use of the available light.

Far right top: Some plants, such as this white foxglove (*Digitalis purpurea albiflora*), grow along the margins of woods where they receive sun for at least part of the day.

Far right bottom: The vegetation changes as you enter the wood, with few plants growing in the densest shade in the middle of the trees.

ground, a few fields say, that has been abandoned by a farmer. At first the grass grows and small flowering plants start to appear. Gradually the ranker vegetation takes over with taller grasses and tough plants, such as thistles and docks, swamping all the more delicate plants. Brambles also spread quickly and the first trees germinate and begin to appear among the smaller plants. Quick-growing trees, such as birch, are one of the earliest to appear in many parts of the globe. As these grow, they in turn swamp the brambles and grasses, their leaves not leaving enough light for these to survive underneath them. Other larger, slower-growing trees now begin to germinate and grow up through the smaller trees. They will eventually tower over them, eliminating them and the other plants below. The climax is reached when the area is covered with perpetual woodland, with little growing beneath it except in special areas where light is able to reach the forest floor.

It is instructive to look at the profile of such a mature woodland as it can teach us a great deal about gardening in the shade. As you approach the wood, there is an abundance of herbaceous vegetation, along with a few shrubs and small trees. These have plenty of light as they are not overshadowed by the larger trees, although they may only receive direct sunlight for part of the day. As you come up closer to the wood, the branches of the trees often sweep down low to the ground, making the maximum use of all available light. Smaller plants grow up to and under these low branches, but they are often different plants to those that are out in the more open areas as they are plants that will survive in the dappled shade found there. Pushing through the branches, you enter the wood itself. Here the tree leaves form a dense canopy and direct sunlight is very restricted, with just occasional beams thrusting through to the

woodland floor. Very little grows in such very shady conditions. As you walk through the wood, however, you will from time to time come across a tree that has fallen over through old age, has been struck down by lightning or has simply been blown over by strong winds. Here the sunlight will stream into the gap left by the fallen tree. The underlying vegetation will have made the most of this, with grasses, ferns and flowering plants appearing in abundance. The same is true of any access rides that have been cut through the trees by land owners. To keep the access open, these rides are often mown regularly preventing many plants growing there, but the edges will be full of plants, reminiscent of the woodland edge itself.

The various areas and different densities of shade, and the types of plants that will survive under these varying conditions, need to be studied in more detail.

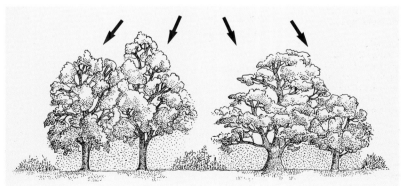

OPEN SHADE

From the gardening point of view, open shade is probably the most important type of shade as it is here that most of the more interesting plants will grow and it is also possibly the most common type of shade found in gardens. Here we are concerned with areas that are not actually covered from above but are in the shadow of buildings, shrubs, hedges, fences or walls. Plenty of light falls to the ground but it is not bright direct sunlight which is kept at bay. In some situations, north-facing ones for example, there may be a glimpse of the sun at some time during the day, such as early in the morning or late in the evening.

In open shade, the conditions are not ideal but they are still better than being in covered shade. This is the equivalent to the approaches to the wood mentioned above, as well as the shady side of a hedge or rocky outcrop. There are plenty of plants from around the world that will grow in these conditions, perhaps not quite so colorful as many that grow in full sun, but still enough to make an interesting display.

Open conditions also occur during the winter and early spring months in deciduous woodlands. Once the canopy has been left open by the dropping of leaves during the fall, much more light can reach the ground, including some direct sunlight. Many plants take advantage of this and what at other times of year may be a barren woodland floor can be carpeted by masses of colorful plants. Wood anemones (*Anemone nemorosa*), bluebells (*Hyacinthoides*

non-scripta) and snowdrops (*Galanthus*) are three well-known examples of plants which exploit this brief period of light on the woodland floor. Their life-cycle above ground is brief compared to other plants as they have adapted themselves perfectly to these conditions. They appear very early in the year, flower, build up reserves for the following year, seed and die back underground all in a couple of months, making the most use of their brief glimpse of the sun.

This opportunity can be exploited by the gardener by growing a wide range of this type of plant under shrubs and trees, areas that are available for use during the winter and spring, but are covered up later on by the developing foliage. It is one way of making maximum use of your garden, especially if it is a small one.

The open shady places to be found on the north sides of buildings or in the angles of walls are often the most troublesome areas that face many gardeners. These areas rarely, if ever, get sun, are much colder than the rest of the garden and frequently seem to be swept by wind. There are many woodland plants that grow in such places: foliage plants such as hostas and ferns are an obvious choice, but there are also many plants that are usually grown for the color of their flowers. For example, orange or yellow *Meconopsis cambrica*, Welsh poppy, will cheer up such an area in the garden from spring well into fall.

Above: Hostas will happily grow in open shade. The variegated forms are useful as they brighten up what could otherwise be a dull corner.

Top: Hydrangeas are perfect plants for open shade as long as the ground is not too dry.

Left: Enchanting bluebells, *Hyacinthoides non-scripta*, cover the woodland floor before the light is excluded by the opening leaves above.

PLANTS FOR UNDER-PLANTING DECIDUOUS TREES

Anemone blanda
Anemone nemorosa
Anemonella thalictroides
Brunnera macrophylla
Caltha palustris
Cardamine bulbifera
Cardamine enneaphyllos
Cardamine heptaphylla
Cardamine pentaphyllos
Chionodoxa
Convallaria majalis
Cornus canadensis
Daphne mezereum
Dicentra
Epimedium
Eranthis hyemalis
Erythronium
Euphorbia amygdaloides
Galanthus
Glaucidium palmatum
Hacquetia epipactis
Helleborus
Hyacinthoides non-scripta
Hydrastis canadensis
Jeffersonia diphylla
Jeffersonia dubia
Lamium galeobdolon
Lamium orvala
Lathyrus vernus
Narcissus
Omphalodes cappadocica
Omphalodes verna
Oxalis acetosella
Primula, polyanthus
Primula vulgaris
Pulmonaria
Sanguinaria canadensis
Smilacina racemosa
Smilacina stellata
Smyrnium perfoliatum
Vancouveria

LIGHT, DAPPLED SHADE

The next level of shade that is suitable for garden use is light, dappled shade. Here the ground is covered by branches from trees or shrubs, but they only cast a light shade. It may be that the leaves are small or thinly distributed, allowing plenty of light to filter through. Sun may penetrate the canopy, constantly shifting as it moves across the sky and as the branches move in the wind. In the garden such places may be under trees, especially tall trees, where the lower branches have been removed, allowing in the sunlight. It may well be in a shrub border where the gaps between shrubs only receive a small amount of direct light. It may also be under a pergola or other area that has been covered with a climbing plant, such as a vine or rose.

There is a large number of plants that will grow in these conditions, but they are nearly all woodland plants. Brightly-colored impatiens and begonias (*Begonia semperflorens*) will both tolerate such conditions, indeed the former prefers a lightly-shaded position. Many lilies will grow in such places and a patch growing amongst shrubs can produce dramatic impact. However very few plants that prefer an open situation can be grown in this shady position.

Having said that, it is possible to grow plants in pots and move them into such conditions for a short while. For example there may be a sitting area covered with a vine producing dappled shade perfect for entertaining. A few pots of bright geraniums or petunias could be introduced for a day or so for a special occasion.

Right: A typical garden with light dappled shade provided by apple trees. The trees provide shade for relaxation as well as a habitat for many shade-loving plants.

Far right: The drumstick primula, *Primula denticulata*, adds both a touch of color and an interesting form to a spring border in dappled shade.

PROBLEM AREAS

In larger cities and surrounding suburbs, houses are generally built close together, often with a concrete path running between the fence and each house, leading to a back garden gate. Usually there is a ribbon of soil along the edge of the path that receives minimal sun — about an hour a day in the height of summer. Most home owners just top-dress the soil with rocks or leave it free for moss and weeds to grow on.

With good soil preparation, it is possible to grow a mixture of low-growing perennials in such a bed. Some examples are creeping jenny (Lysimachia nummularia 'Aurea'), with its ground-hugging golden leaves that seem to glow on overcast days; silver-leaved forms of Lamium maculatum; Ajuga reptans, which creeps along the soil; and Pulmonaria longifolia 'Bertram Anderson' with silver-spotted leaves. Probably none of them will bloom in such conditions, but with such tex-tured and colorful foliage, they will please the eye as long as they are fed and watered from time to time.

If contained in a small bed (and contained is emphasized), variegated Aegopodium podagraria 'Variegatum' really brightens up a shady corner. For an even more stunning effect, try mixing another invasive ground cover with it, sweet woodruff (Galium odoratum). The frothy white flowers mixed with the lighter variegated foliage is like a giant wedding bouquet.

MEDIUM SHADE

Moving deeper into the shade, it is still possible to grow a number of lovely plants that can make a contribution to the garden. Here there is still quite a lot of light but little direct sunlight. It may be a path through a wooded area, where the trees are almost closed high above, but there is little immediate vegetation that densely shades the ground. Here the plants are not likely to be particularly colorful in flower, yellow or white being typical colors, but many are valuable for their foliage effect, such as hostas.

Shade will often affect a plant's ability to flower. While it may grow happily in medium shade, it will sometimes be shy of flowering. For example, the lesser periwinkle (*Vinca minor*) is often quoted as a plant for medium shade. It will indeed grow in these conditions, but it will only throw up the occasional flower, while in a more sunny position, it will be covered in flowers. Fortunately it, and many other plants like it, are valuable for their foliage alone and are worth growing in medium shade.

DEEP SHADE

Dense shade is one of the worst areas for the gardener, but fortunately it is not a very common situation unless you have a large wood, or a tree such as beech or horse chestnut in the garden. These huge trees have a dense canopy of leaves through which both light and rain have difficulty penetrating and thus the two vital ingredients that a plant requires for growth are missing. Possibly the worse form of dense shade is produced by evergreen trees and shrubs. Here so much light is excluded that it can be quite gloomy and sometimes almost dark. Holly, yew and the likes are the trees to avoid here. Conifers, too, generally are bad news if you want to be able to grow plants under them.

The problem is that very little will grow under these conditions. This is not only due to the fact that sunlight cannot penetrate, but, as we will see later, neither can rain; it runs off the leaves to be shed round the outside of the tree, leaving the area immediately under it very dry. Conditions are so barren that not even grass can be grown, but consolation can be drawn from the fact that it is rarely necessary to weed in such places! One of the few plants that can survive under such circumstances, as long as it is not too dark, is *Cyclamen hederifolium*, a delightful plant that is well worth cultivating. Another is ivy, which will grow in a wider range of climatic zones and will form a rich carpet of decorative foliage.

If the trees are deciduous, it is quite

possible to grow some early-flowering plants, such as wood anemones, as long as the soil is not too dry. Adding plenty of well-rotted organic matter will help matters considerably.

A small patch of dense shade, such as that under one tree, can normally be left to itself. However in a small garden it can represent a substantial portion of the area available. If possible without spoiling the shape of the tree, trim off some of the lower branches to allow in more light and rain. If the tree is deciduous, try growing winter and early-flowering spring plants under it so that it is successful during one season. One way of making it useful is to place a seat around the tree and use it as a shady sitting place in warm weather. Mulch the soil with shredded bark for a neat appearance. Or if there are children about, turn it into a play area with a climbing frame or tree house.

Far left: In light to medium shade, arrange plants in drifts on a generous scale. Dot planting looks out of place. Here, *Rhododendron* 'Sappho' forms an elegant backdrop to ostrich ferns (*Matteuccia*) and rodgersia.

Left: Ivy is an ideal ground cover for medium or deep shade. It makes interesting shapes when grown over objects or uneven ground.

Above: A dark, damp spot where few flowering plants will grow, but a mixture of ferns, moss and ground-covering periwinkle (*Vinca*) makes an interesting picture.

SOME PLANTS FOR MEDIUM SHADE

Achlys triphylla

Actaea

Allium ursinum

Arum italicum

Asarum

Carex pendula

Cyclamen coum

Cyclamen hederifolium

Dryopteris filix-mas

Epimedium

Euphorbia amygdaloides robbiae

Galanthus

Geranium

Hedera helix

Hosta

Iris foetidissima

Lamium galeobdolon

Lonicera pileata

Pachysandra

Polygonatum

Polystichum setiferum

Rubus tricolor

Ruscus aculeatus

Stylophorum

Tellima grandiflora

Trillium

Uvularia

Vancouveria

Vinca minor

Waldsteinia ternata

PLANTS FOR DEEPER SHADE

Aucuba japonica

Buxus

Cyclamen hederifolium

Daphne laureola

Hedera

Hosta

Ruscus aculeatus

Skimmia

MOISTURE, HUMIDITY AND TEMPERATURE

Trees and shrubs are very thirsty plants and remove great quantities of water from the soil every day. This means that any herbaceous plants that grow under them, particularly under shallow-rooted trees, are in direct competition. Thus the area immediately below the tree is likely to be naturally quite dry. However, the soil beneath a tree is usually covered with a deep layer of leaf litter, leaves in various states of decay. Leaf litter is the perfect medium for holding mois-

always be borne in mind when planting close to such objects.

Sometimes, rain will be partly directed inward and the water runs down the branches and onto the trunk. Frequently this follows the same course each times it rains and its line is clearly marked by a green flush of algae and moss. On the ground it will flow away from the tree, often along the same channel and this will create a linear oasis under the tree where plants can thrive.

Moist leafmold often creates a microclimate under trees and shrubs

ture and most woodland plants tend to grow in it. If the area under the tree has been swept clear of fallen leaves, either by the wind or by the gardener, it loses this moist layer and plants have difficulty competing with the tree roots for what little moisture there is.

The situation can be further complicated by the way the rain is blown against the tree. In an exposed position, a strong wind may blow plenty of moisture under the tree, but leave a dry area on the far side beyond the boundaries of the tree. This may well be a problem with hedges, walls and fences, which create a rain 'shadow' on their leeward side. This must

where the air is kept quite moist compared with that out in the sun and wind. A plant that grows happily in such woodland conditions may well be stressed if planted in the open where water loss from its leaves will now be much greater than its uptake through the roots.

A similar situation occurs with temperature. The enclosed environment means that there is far less fluctuation than out in the open. Again a woodland plant may find high summer temperatures too much for healthy growth, while winter temperatures may be too low, especially without insulating leafmold covering its roots.

Above: Rain falling on a tree will drain off the leaves toward the perimeter of the canopy, leaving the area below the tree relatively dry. Rain accompanied by prevailing winds will leave a 'rain shadow' on the lee of a tree or hedge.

Right: Cyclamen hederifolium will grow in the inhospitable conditions of both shade and dry soil.

The soil in woodlands can vary as much as the soil does anywhere else. The underlying soil is obviously that of the area, depending on whatever the geological structure might be. However, the topsoil will be conditioned by the wood itself. In an old established wood, the natural soil may well be covered with a thick layer of topsoil created over generations by the falling and rotting of leaves.

The woodland cycle allows for the leaves of the trees to fall to the ground at least once a year. In the case of deciduous trees this is in the fall. Evergreen trees, contrary to popular belief, also drop their leaves, but not necessarily all at once, and so it is less conspicuous. The fallen leaves rot down, enriching the soil with the nutrients that they contain, as well as providing fibrous material that is exceptionally good at holding moisture, and yet not becoming waterlogged. This is the soil that most plants would relish if it were not for the shade cast from the trees above, as it is only those that have learned to cope with the light limitations that enjoy it. As well as being the perfect conditions for plant life, insects and other small animals revel in it.

In some woods and especially under isolated trees, the ground may be swept clean by strong winds. In which

soil and shade

Soil is the most important factor in a garden. Get that right and everything else will fall into place. Although some aspects are beyond our control, others are well within our means, such as improving the general condition of the soil.

case the soil can become impoverished with the tree or trees becoming stunted and with very little growing beneath them. Avoid this in the garden. Do not sweep up leaves in shady areas. If the garden is windswept and there is the possibility that all the leaves will end up in your neighbor's garden, sweep them up before they

disappear, rot them down in a leafmold bin (see page 29) and return it to the soil once it has been broken down. Do not go to your nearest wood and remove the leafmold to use in your garden, as it will break the wood's natural cycle and do the trees a great harm.

The degree of acidity or alkalinity of woodland soil will vary according to the local soil. Leafmold has a tendency towards acidity, but that on chalky soils may well be alkaline. Conifers usually produce an acid leafmold wherever they grow, but this will not be strong enough on chalky soils to counteract the natural alkalinity and will certainly not be sufficient to allow you to grow rhododendrons and azaleas.

Woodland soils are very often dry, as explained in the last chapter, partly because of the way rainfall is shed and partly because of the moisture the trees draw up and expel. If it were not for the moisture-retentive leafmold, many plants would not be able to survive. In some woods there is often an area, usually lower than the rest, which is damp, sometimes boggy or even with a pond. Not many trees will grow in boggy conditions, willow (*Salix*) and bald cypress (*Taxodium distichum*) being the main exceptions.

Far left: Beechwoods and other woods that have existed in the same place for many years build up a deep layer of leafmold which is cool, moist and full of nutrients: the ideal soil for many of the shade-loving plants.

Above right: Scilla mischtschenkoana breaking through a layer of chipped bark, which forms an effective substitute for a woodland layer of leafmold.

CREATING WOODLAND CONDITIONS IN THE GARDEN

If one intends to grow shade-loving plants in the garden, then it is essential to create the right sort of soil conditions. Generally, these conditions are the same as described above: rich in moisture-retaining leafmold. If you are lucky enough to have a wood, even a small one, then the conditions may naturally occur, but in many garden situations it will have to be provided, especially when the shade is produced by man-made objects such as buildings, which obviously make no contribution to the soil, unlike woodland.

The most natural way is to add leafmold. This should be home made (see page 29) and not taken from a local wood. However, any well-rotted organic material will do. Garden compost is ideal, as is farmyard manure as long as it does not contain too much weed seed. Spent mushroom compost is another soil conditioner that is available in some areas, but if you want to grow rhododendrons and other ericaceous plants, it should be used with caution as it generally contains chalk or lime, both of which will kill such plants.

These materials can be dug into the top soil or can simply be used as a mulch. Another natural material that is usually used purely as a mulch is shredded bark. A layer of about 4 inches spread over the surface will not only help to keep moisture in and provide a cool root-run for plants, but will also help to condition the soil as it gradually breaks down. Keep any mulch well topped up by adding fresh material during the fall and spring every year, if possible. Do not use peat as this breaks down too quickly and is liable to blow away as it dries out. Also, peat resources are under threat from over-extraction, so it should not really be used for this reason alone.

The other material that should not be used is leafy soil removed from a local wood. Although it may seem an obvious free source of material, removing it will break the woodland's cycle and impoverish it considerably.

MULCHES AND SOIL CONDITIONERS

BLACK PLASTIC	*Good but ugly mulch, no use as a soil conditioner*
CHIPPED OR SHREDDED BARK	*Excellent*
COCO SHELLS	*Attractive mulch, but are slow to rot*
FARMYARD MANURE	*Excellent, but can contain weed seed*
GARDEN COMPOST	*Excellent*
GRASS CLIPPINGS	*Good if not used too thickly*
GRAVEL	*Good mulch, good conditioner for clay soils*
SAWDUST	*Unattractive, but good mulch*
SHREDDED LEAVES	*The best*
SEAWEED	*Excellent*
PEANUT, RICE OR COTTONSEED HULLS	*Unattractive, but good mulch and soil conditioner*
PEAT	*Avoid*
PINE NEEDLES	*Very good*
SPENT MUSHROOM COMPOST	*Very good, but may contain chalk*
STRAW	*Good, but unsightly*

Above: Gravel can be an attractive mulch. It looks more natural in open shade rather than in a woodland setting, where bark or leafmold would be more appropriate.

It will take years, possibly centuries to build up again to a similar depth.

Grass cuttings are a good substitute for leafmold. They can either be composted in bins and then spread on the ground, or spread directly. Do not use too deep a layer or it will be very slow to break down. If necessary, turn it occasionally with a fork to allow air to enter and prevent it becoming a slimy mass. Worms quickly incorporate it into the soil, making the soil richer. Grass cuttings, however, do not look very attractive so if the bed is in a prominent position, spread them toward the back and let the birds gradually scatter them through the bed in a way that is hardly noticeable.

MULCHING

Above: Water the ground before adding a mulch. The mulch must be at least 4 inches deep. Tuck it around the plants but avoid covering them.

27

Right: Blue poppies, like this *Meconopsis* x *sheldonii*, are some of the most exquisite woodland plants. They like a rich soil and are perfect for a peat bed.

Far right: A lush primula nestling in deep, cool leafmold.

PEAT BEDS

The avoidance of peat raises the question of raised "peat" beds. One way of avoiding the problem of invasive tree roots when planting under a tree is to build a raised bed. These are usually in the shade, but sometimes extend out into the more sunny areas. Traditionally these beds were built up much in the manner of a rock garden, except that the walls or ledges were made of peat blocks and the soil infill was a mixture of good garden soil and peat. These are excellent places for growing a wide range of plants, including dwarf rhododendrons and azaleas. Nowadays, raised beds are still constructed but not using peat. The retaining walls are made with logs of wood and the infill uses other organic material, such as leafmold or well-rotted garden compost, along with the garden loam. Unfortunately the tree's roots will eventually move up to take advantage of the moisture and nutrients in the raised bed and it will need renewing.

The best time for planting such a bed is in the fall at about the time of leaf-fall. This will allow the new plants some time to establish themselves before the onset of a new canopy of leaves overhead in the spring and will give the plants a stretch of time when the weather is comfortably cool and rainfall is plentiful so they can become established before winter.

While it is preferable to solve the moisture problem in shady areas by modifying the soil to turn it into a leafy, moisture-retentive soil, it is of course possible to solve it simply by watering, and this may be essential

1. To make a leafmold bin, bend a strip of wire mesh to form a circle. Entwine the ends to hold the circle firm.

2. Slip four canes through the mesh and push them into the ground, equally spaced around the bin.

3. Fill the bin and press down. Repeat until full.

4. After 1–2 years, remove the crumbly leafmold.

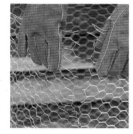

anyway in some areas. Under trees, watering can be a rather laborious task. Everything needs a good soak to make it worthwhile and it needs to be done regularly. Methods of watering are dealt with later, but apart from localized watering for newly-planted plants or for very small areas, it is not a job that can be carried out with a watering can. Some form of drip-hose or other automatic watering system would be the best.

MAKING LEAFMOLD

Of all materials available to the gardener the most valuable when trying to create a shade garden or shade border is leafmold. It is formed naturally as leaves that have fallen in the fall decay. In the wild this happens either on the woodland floor where they have fallen or in drifts where the wind has blown them. In the garden, the leaves that fall from hedgerows, trees and shrubs often

tend to fall in places where they are unwanted or look unsightly, such as on lawns or on paths which then become slippery and dangerous.

Traditionally, many gardeners have swept up and burned the leaves. While the smoke may produce a smell wonderfully evocative of fall, this is a tremendous waste of a useful natural resource. The leaves should be swept up and then placed in a wire netting bin where they can rot down. Leaves are slow in rotting and may take one to two years before they have broken down enough to be used as a mulch or soil conditioner. Once the leaves have broken down and have turned into a dark, rich crumbly mass they are ready to use. They can be spread as a mulch on the shade beds or can be dug in to help condition the soil in any area of the garden.

Most gardens are too small to produce enough leaves to make any decent quantity of leafmold, but it is

1. A slatted wooden bin is best for making compost. It allows air to circulate through the material.

2. Add the material, shredding or breaking down woody matter if necessary. Alternate layers of coarse and fine matter.

3. Cover the top of the bin with a plastic bag to keep in the heat.

4. The compost will be ready to use within a few months.

often possible to obtain leaves from neighbors who are unaware of their value and are only too willing to dispose of them. Many civic authorities still dump fallen leaves and are prepared to give them away, but make sure they come from parks and not from the roadside as they may be polluted and will harm your plants.

As already mentioned, what you should not do is to remove either leaves or leafmold from woods or forests as this will upset the natural cycle and if carried out for several years could do irreparable harm by removing vital nutrients.

In addition, or as an alternative, garden compost is well worth making and using. For garden compost, it is better to use bins that are more substantial, ones with wooden slats being ideal. It is worth making three compost bins. One for adding material to, one which is in the process of rotting down and one from which to be taking the ready compost. For the small garden, commercially-made bins can be purchased in which the new ingredients are added to the top and the ready compost is taken out at the base, reducing the necessity of having three bins. Others are designed like

cement mixers, allowing the contents to be tumbled daily, which can make compost in as little as three weeks.

All garden refuse, except pernicious weeds and anything in seed, can be added. Woody material should first be shredded, cut up very fine or be broken up with a hammer. Any uncooked vegetable kitchen waste can also be added. Add the material as it becomes available and turn the contents of the heap occasionally. It is ready once it has all broken down, but still has a fibrous texture. Good garden compost should not have an unpleasant smell when it is ready.

Far left: In dry gardens such as this, it is essential to add as much well-rotted compost to the soil as possible to keep plants growing this well.

Left: Mulches, such as leafmold, act as a background and a perfect foil to set off foliage and flowers alike.

INSTANT LEAFMOLD

If you don't have the space or time to make proper leafmold, here is a quick way to achieve similar results. Get a large garbage can, fill it two-thirds full with dry leaves, put an electric weed cutter in and whizz it around a few times. This soon breaks the leaves down and you have instant leafmold, which can be worked into the soil immediately or bagged and stored for use in the spring.

31

Above: Christmas box (*Sarcococca hookeriana digyna*) is a useful plant for dry shade. Its fragrant flowers appear at Christmas. Plant near a path to appreciate it.

Above right: The lilyturf, *Liriope muscari*, flowers in the fall with its stiff purple flower spikes.

DRY SHADE

Dry shade is probably the most difficult area with which the gardener has to contend. The problem is that not many plants are willing to grow under these conditions, and many of those that do grow there are not particularly exciting.

The best approach is to try and change the conditions. Start by opening up the bottom of the tree if it is possible, by removing some of the lower branches to let the rain blow in and to allow more light to reach the ground. Next look to the soil. Dig it deep and add as much organic matter as you possibly can as this will help the soil to become moisture retaining. When the bed has been prepared, water very thoroughly and then add a deep layer of leafmold or other organic material on top. This mulch should be at least + inches deep to be really effective.

PLANTS FOR DRY SHADE

Aucuba japonica
Alchemilla mollis
Carex pendula
Cyclamen cyprium
Cyclamen hederifolium
Dryopteris filix-mas
Epimidium × versicolor
Euonymus japonicus
Euphorbia amygdaloides robbiae
Helleborus foetidus
Liriope muscari
Lonicera pileata
Polystichum setiferum
Rubus tricolor
Ruscus aculeatus
Sarcococca
Vancouveria
Vinca difformis
Vinca minor
Waldsteinia ternata

Right: Aucuba is a valuable plant for dry shade as its bright leaves seem to lighten a dull spot.

This will work very well for beds shaded by walls, but in beds created under thirsty trees there could still be a problem as the trees will quickly grab any moisture and nutrients that you manage to add there. The deeper the mulch the better chance there is of being able to grow woodland plants such as trilliums in it. It may be necessary to water the area regularly, especially in dry weather. Installing a drip-feed hose that releases a constant but slight dribble of water into the soil surrounding it is a labor-saving solution to this common problem.

Shade is often seen as a problem area in a garden. However, to the keen gardener it can be seen as a necessity as there are so many garden-worthy plants that can only be grown out of the wilting rays of the sun. For those with grand aspirations and plenty of space it is possible to plant a whole wood, but even those with only a small garden can create a shady area if they have not already got one.

In the tiniest of gardens, a single shrub will produce enough shade for growing a few shade-loving plants. Choose shrubs that produce a light, dappled shade and ones that preferably have deep roots rather than those that run near the surface. Many of the acers are good but avoid the large-leaved forms, especially sycamore (*Acer pseudoplatanus*). Birch (*Betula*) has a good canopy for providing light shade although the roots can be a bit of a nuisance. Oak is ideal when mature as its canopy can be trimmed so that it is high, allowing in just the right amount of light, and its roots are deep. The only problem is that you may have to wait anything up to 100 years for it to reach maturity, although in practical terms it will be a suitable size long before that. The ideal shade-producers are apple trees (*Malus*). An area in a garden shaded by one apple tree makes a superb

creating shade

If you don't have any shade in the garden, why not create some? It will not only give you somewhere to relax, but also provide habitats to allow you to grow a wider range of plants. Even a single shrub will create a miniature shade garden.

place to grow shade-loving plants. If you have a tree that is no longer producing fruit in any quantity, do not be tempted to cut it down, use it as the basis of a shade bed. The big, old-fashioned standard apple trees are the best, although in a small garden something on a dwarfed rootstock will probably be more suitable.

There are plenty of deciduous shrubs that are suitable for casting shade in which to grow early shade-loving plants such as wood anemones (*Anemone nemorosa* and *A. blanda*) and bluebells (*Hyacinthoides non-scripta*) which appear and die back before the shrub comes into leaf. Once the leaves appear the shrub is too close to the ground for any further use but a collection of shrubs will produce shady areas between them which are ideal for many plants that like open or light shade.

When choosing trees and shrubs, think of all their characteristics. Some, for example, produce colorful flowers, perhaps with an attractive scent. Others produce wonderful fall color or attractive berries or fruit. During the winter when there are no leaves, handsome bark comes into its own.

There are some trees and shrubs that are best avoided. Evergreens are likely to produce shade that is too dense and should be avoided for their shade potential, although, of course, they have other characteristics that make them useful plants to have in a garden. Another type of plant that, although decorative in the garden, is no good as a shade producing plant is the fastigiate or columnar trees and shrubs. An extreme example would

Far left: The combination of bluebells and azaleas blooming together in late spring is a popular one for a woodland garden and it is easy to see why.

Above right: Different tree shapes create different amounts of shade. The tree on the far right provides the largest area of usable shade.

it out!). Beech (*Fagus sylvatica*) trees are both dense in terms of shade and very dry. As well as having a thick canopy, one of the reasons for this is that the branches often sweep right down to the ground, allowing neither light nor rain to come in from the side. Any trees that have this tendency should be avoided. Do check a tree's ultimate size; it may get there beyond your lifetime, but it is still worth checking that the tree you want to grow is not too big for the garden space available. Another problem that is worth anticipating is that some trees, lime (*Tilia*) in particular, produce a great deal of sooty honeydew that coats everything black. This is not a tree for the small garden. Also remember to avoid planting too close

be the Lombardy poplar (*Populus nigra* 'Italica'), which can be very tall but very narrow and casts very little useful shade. Many of the willows (*Salix*) produce a delicate shade that is suitable from the light point of view

but have roots that are not only very close to the surface, thus making it difficult to dig, but that are very thirsty and quickly mop up any moisture that there is around (they are often planted on boggy ground to dry

SHADE FOR COLD CLIMATES

Here are three often overlooked but very hardy shade trees that will not become too unwieldy in the average garden. Prunus virginiana 'Schubert' reaches no more than 20–25 feet in height. It has beautiful pale spring blossoms followed by fresh new green leaves that turn to a wine color by midsummer and a dramatic purple-red by the time fall arrives.

Bur oak (Quercus macrocarpa) is a perfect candidate for extremely cold areas (zone 2). It has attractive round oak leaves in mid green and the acorn cups have a most handsome mossy appearance, almost like the stems of a moss rose. Its ultimate height is anything up to about 80 feet, but in cold climates it is very slow growing, mak-

ing it the perfect choice of shade tree for a small garden.

The Manchurian cherry (Prunus maackii) is also often disregarded as a shade tree because of its height (33–42 feet). Its smooth, cinnamon-

colored bark is a beautiful feature in the winter months when it is most visible. The shiny nature of the bark makes it appear to glow. This tree makes an especially good specimen if purchased multi-trunked.

Right: Manchurian Cherry (*Prunus maackii*) makes a fine specimen for even a small garden. The shiny bark really comes to the fore when the leaves begin to drop in fall.

to buildings as the tree roots may undermine the foundations. In fact, there is legislation in some areas of the country to avoid this happening.

Container-grown trees and shrubs can theoretically be planted at any time of year, as long as the ground is not frozen. But in hot and windy weather, the stress caused in particular by water-loss can be too great. Early fall is generally the best time, giving plants time to get established before winter. Bare root plants, on the other hand, are better planted in spring in most areas. If you have to plant out of the normal period, make certain that the plants are watered thoroughly until established, and protected from drying winds. It is also best to avoid planting in waterlogged soils; wait until the soil dries out before attempting to even dig it over.

Normally when planting a tree or shrub, you would just dig the area immediately around the planting hole, enriching it with well-rotted organic material. But since you are hoping to grow shade-loving plants under the tree or shrub, it is well worth preparing the whole area, adding as much organic material as you possibly can.

Stake trees and taller shrubs after planting. They should be tied, with proper tree ties, about 12 inches from the ground so that the rootball is held firmly in place and not allowed to rock. The top of the tree should be allowed to sway in the wind. In windy positions, place windbreak netting round the tree to prevent it drying out or being damaged. A guard round the trunk may also be necessary to protect from animals. Water well until the tree or shrub has become established. Mulching around it helps to preserve the moisture as well as keeping competing weeds at bay.

SUITABLE TREES FOR CREATING SHADE

Acer

Betula

Malus

Prunus

Quercus

Sorbus

SOME SHRUBS FOR CREATING SHADE

Acer

Amelanchier

Buddleja

Cornus

Corylopsis

Corylus

Cotinus

Deutzia

Exochorda

Forsythia

Hamamelis

Lonicera, shrubby forms

Rhododendron, deciduous azaleas

Ribes

Tamarix

Above, right and far right: Drive the stake into the planting hole before planting a tree. Ensure the top of the rootball is level with the soil surface. Support the trunk with an adjustable tree tie, about 12 inches above the ground. Water well, then mulch around the tree.

ARTIFICIAL SHADE

Trees and shrubs can take several years to get established, a long time if you are keen to get on with creating a shade garden. However, it is possible to create some form of artificial shade. There is a variety of different types of shade netting sold by garden centers, nurseries and special outlets, that is mainly used for screening greenhouses and cold frames. It can be bought in different strengths, some producing almost total shade while others, with a much wider mesh, creating only a light shade.

For the shade gardener, this netting is ideal. It can be erected horizontal on short stakes to allow plants to be shaded while the recently-planted tree or shrub can grow unimpeded through a hole in it. When the trees or shrubs are large enough to provide enough shade, the netting can be removed.

Such structures are not particularly attractive in the border and some gardeners may prefer to wait until the natural shade has grown big enough, before they plant underneath it. However, this waiting time need not be wasted. One of the best and most natural ways of planting up a shady area is with drifts of plants. These, if bought in quantity, can be very expensive, but with time on his side the gardener can set about producing plenty of his own plants. For this he will require a shade frame in which to grow and store the plants in their pots, as they cannot be left out in the

Above right: A large clump of hosta, such as this *Hosta* 'Spinners', can be divided, potted up and grown on in a shade frame until the pieces are large enough to be planted out in the garden.

Right: Shade netting can be attached to a simple wooden frame to make a shade frame.

Far right: A shade frame will provide space to house shade-loving plants waiting to be planted out, preventing them being scorched by the sun. It is also a good place to raise seeds and cuttings.

Left: Growing trees and shrubs to provide shade can be a long-term project. While waiting for them to grow, there is no reason why you could not plant up a bed like this one and protect the plants with shade netting until the trees are large enough to cast shade of their own.

full sun or the leaves will become scorched and the plants will wither.

A shade frame is a wooden structure covered with the same netting as previously described. The frame could be an old greenhouse with the glass removed, or it could be a pur-pose-built frame, made from uprights set in the ground connected with horizontal bars. The structure should be tall enough to walk through, but a cheaper structure can be made with the netting suspended just above the pots. In this case it will have to be removed every time the pots are attended to. Low-level shade can also be constructed in the manner of a cold frame with the netting being stretched over the openings instead of glass. A lath house is another alternative, popular in many areas.

Right: A pergola covered with roses, clematis and wisteria. By choosing plants that flower at different times, the pergola has interest over a long period.

PERGOLAS AND WALKWAYS

One of the most exciting ways of using shade is in a decorative way. Rather than rely on trees and shrubs, or the more sterile shade netting, climbers are used in a controlled way to create walkways or even, as we will see later, sitting areas.

Pergolas help the design of a garden in many ways. They provide vertical interest, breaking up what might be a flat expanse of garden. They can act as screens, just allowing glimpses of the garden beyond, thus creating an air of mystery and making the garden appear larger than it is. What might be boring paths can be enlivened and made more interesting. Finally, and more in keeping with our subject, they provide shade, both for the human that passes along them and for the plants that are planted underneath them.

Remember to take into account the eventual width of the plants when building the pergola and make it wide and tall so that the plants do not catch on people as they walk through.

Also allow enough space to plant along the side of the path in the shade of the pergola. For special occasions, tubs of colorful sun-loving plants can be moved into the shade or positioned at the entrance and exit of the tunnel.

Quite a number of climbing plants, clematis being a prime example, while liking to have their heads in the sun, prefer to have their bases in shade. These make ideal plants for pergolas. Most plants prefer to flower in the sun and these are more likely to appear on the outside of the pergola, although those on a lightly-clad pergola will be seen from the inside as well. When choosing plants, it is well to avoid roses with thorns such as 'Albertine'; choose one that has few thorns or one that is completely thornless like 'Zéphirine Drouhin'.

One of the simplest pergolas consists of a series of vertical posts set in the ground with cross bars over the top and along the length, just like a series of arches. More ornate ones can be created using brick pillars. It is possible to buy commercially-made pergolas made from steel tubing. These are suitable for the small garden, but tend to be a bit too narrow and short for larger gardens.

Right: Pergolas can be bought as ready-made kits, or can be tailor made. Wooden pergolas should be treated with a preservative and the nails should be galvanized.

1. A basic pergola consists of four uprights fixed securely into the ground. The side bars slot into channels in the tops.

2. The cross pieces are also notched. These fit over the side bars.

3. Arrange the cross pieces at regular intervals along the side bars.

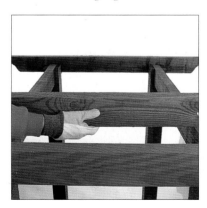

Below: A truly magnificent walkway covered in grape vines. Not only is this pleasant to walk through, but it provides a perfect habitat for ferns and other shade-loving plants.

Pergolas are usually enclosed walkways but it is equally possible to have ones that are not covered over the top. These are not so shady but still pleasant to walk through. One of the easiest to construct is to place two parallel rows of poles in the ground, one along either side of the path, and link the tops of the poles along each row with a thick rope, allowing it to sag slightly between the poles. Climbers can then be grown up the poles and along the ropes, creating swags of foliage and blooms.

While pergolas are usually used for shading a path, they can be constructed in such a way that they can be used for growing shade-loving plants. Make them wider and just have a small access path running through so that you can both tend and look at the plants. The orientation should be planned as you do not want the pergola to be a wind tunnel, or the plants will undoubtedly suffer. Turn it away from the prevailing wind and avoid placing it where wind is generated between two buildings.

PLANTS SUITABLE FOR PERGOLAS

Akebia

Campsis radicans

Clematis

Humulus

Lonicera

Rosa

Vigna (syn. Phaseolus)

Vitis

41

Above: A custom-built arbor wreathed in the fragrant rose 'Alister Stella Gray' provides a magical, shady place to sit on a warm day.

ARBORS AND SITTING AREAS

Arbors are not that dissimilar from short pergolas except that although you can walk into them, you cannot walk out the other end. In other words they form a space enclosed on three sides and over the top, in some cases almost like a vegetative cave. They make ideal places for relaxing and are normally big enough to take a bench or some other form of seating. Some may be large enough to accommodate a table as well and can be used for eating and entertaining.

Arbors can be secret, romantic places, perhaps tucked away in an odd corner of the garden, or they can be more obvious, perhaps opening onto a patio or lawn. The covering of plants adds to their atmosphere, especially if they include scented flowers, such as roses or honeysuckle (*Lonicera*). There is no need to stick to one type of plant: honeysuckle, roses and clematis, for example, can all be mixed together, extending the season of interest.

They need not be complicated structures and can be easily made. One of the simplest ways is to buy four panels of trellis and some posts, using three panels for the sides and the fourth for the top. The plants are then allowed to ramble over it. Unless they are well tucked away, avoid roses with thorns.

It is possible to create an arbor with no structure at all, simply by "carving" it out of an existing large bush, or by planting several shrubs and training them to form a "cave."

Another type of shady area can be created for eating and entertaining. This consists purely of a canopy of climbers. Four or six strong posts are placed in the ground and then trellis panels, or poles are attached to make a roof. Plants are allowed to grow up the poles and spread out across the top. This produces a dappled shade but is not enclosed round the edges. Grape vines (*Vitis*) are ideal plants for this as they produce a very pleasant shade on a hot summer's day.

Containers of shade-loving plants can be placed at the entrance to arbors or under dappled shade areas. Large pots of colorful impatiens and begonias could be left permanently in the shade as long as the shade is not too deep.

PLANTS SUITABLE FOR ARBORS

Akebia

Campsis radicans

Clematis

Fallopia baldschuanica

Hedera

Humulus

Lonicera

Rosa

Vigna (syn. *Phaseolus*)

Vitis

Right: A home-made arbor constructed from oddments of timber and bricks immediately looks weathered and well established. This one is large enough to have meals in, shaded by clematis and a grape vine with decorative leaves.

REDUCING SHADE: PRUNING

Sometimes there is just a bit too much shade in a garden, or perhaps some or all of it is a bit too deep. If it is created by trees and shrubs then it may be possible to reduce it by thinning them out. If there are too many trees, all too close together, then it is a good idea, whether you want the shade or not, to thin them out so that each can develop unimpeded. If they are allowed to continue growing too close together, it is possible that none of them will give their full potential, each becoming leggy and distorted.

From the shade point of view, it is also a good thing to thin them out to allow in more light, but with larger trees such as oaks, they will probably soon fill the gaps left by the removal of the other specimens. If you have a large enough garden, thin them to allow for this so that there will always be some light filtering down between the trees to the garden floor.

A more usual way of allowing more light to get down to the plants is to remove some of the lower branches. These should be neatly trimmed almost flush with the trunk. Remember to respect the tree and do not sheer off most of the branches so that it ends up looking like a toilet brush with a tall straight stem and a tuft at the top. If you do this, you will also risk weakening the tree and losing it. With trees and taller shrubs that have multiple stems rather than one main trunk, removing one or more of the stems will improve things, but again, do not wreck the plant's shape.

Trees are an emotive subject and no work should be carried out on them, either cutting them down or severely pruning them, without first checking with the civic authority that you are allowed to do so. Much grief has been caused by people cutting down trees first and asking for permission later, often after neighbors or passers-by have complained.

Safety is another subject that must be taken into account. Do not use dangerous tools such as chain saws unless you have been taught how to use them. Wear the correct clothing, including a hard hat and goggles. Watch out for falling stems and branches, particularly keeping an eye on any children that may come near the area. Keep all tools sharp as they will not only be more efficient but safer to use. If in any doubt at all, get somebody who is qualified to do the job, to either help you or to carry out the work themselves.

Above: Trees can be pruned to let more light reach the plants beneath them. Lower branches can be removed (top) to allow light to enter from the sides; or the canopy can be thinned (bottom) to let light enter from above.

Far left: This area could be turned into a shady bed by removing the shrubs and thinning the tree branches, allowing more light to reach the ground.

Left: To prevent splitting, tree branches should be cut in the following way.

1. First make a cut from the underside, cutting half way through the branch.

2. Now make a cut from the top of the branch to join up with the first cut and free the loose end.

3. Cut close to a side shoot so there is no snag to cause die back.

Right: This small courtyard appears larger than it is by the use of a mirror built into an archway against the wall. It reflects an image of the building opposite, making the arch look like an entrance through to another courtyard. Apart from introducing a feeling of greater space, the mirror also reflects light back at the plants around it.

Far right: White paint has been used to brighten this courtyard. The white walls reflect a surprising amount of light back into the area, making it a brighter place to be and increasing the types of plants that will grow there.

REDUCING SHADE: REFLECTING LIGHT BACK IN

It is not so easy to reduce the shade cast by buildings or walls as it is to prune trees. Occasionally it might be possible to remove or reduce a fence or hedge, but such action can be a bit drastic. One way is to reflect more light into the area concerned. In a small courtyard garden, possibly in a dark basement area, painting at least one wall with white paint will help considerably. If the wall catches the sun, so much the better.

On a more restricted level, it is possible to use a large mirror to reflect the light. This has two advantages. First it throws light back into the darker area and secondly its reflection makes the garden appear to double in size. It is a well-known *trompe-l'oeil* effect. Soften the edge of the mirror by surrounding it with climbing plants or trellising. People will not be expecting a mirror and so it will not be noticed at a quick glance, but the reflection will simply be thought of as being another part of the garden.

Right: Use an exterior grade paint on an outside wall and follow the manufacturer's instructions.

1. Prepare the surface, scraping off loose material. Wash to remove dirt.

2. Paint the wall with a roller or brush, working the paint into all the crevices.

Since there are so many different types of shade situation, there is no one way of designing for shade in general. The layout of plants in a large woodland garden is bound to vary from that of a single bush or from that in a container. The key is to do what looks the most appropriate and in character with the setting. For example, large beds of bright red impatiens would look incongruous in a natural woodland setting. On the other hand, drifts of woodland plants that fit naturally into the landscape create the ideal planting. In Britain, for example, large drifts of bluebells (*Hyacinthoides non-scripta*) are found in the wild in woodlands and thus look perfect there. In Europe, a similar swathe of blue *Aquilegia vulgaris* may be found meandering along the edge of a wood, while in America, trilliums of one species or another will form drifts in the wild.

These big drifts are for the large woodland garden, but they can be copied on a smaller scale. An area under a small *Acer palmatum* can be filled with *Anemone nemorosa* in the early spring, the white dancing flowers showing through the naked branches where in a few weeks the leaves will become so dense that even the dying remains of the anemones cannot be seen.

designing for shade

As with so many aspects of gardening, the best results for shady areas come from a conscious design rather than a haphazard planting. Since your choice of plants will be dictated by the conditions, shade plantings should be as natural as possible.

On a slightly larger scale, a single mature oak tree will provide an ideal space for a wonderful woodland bed. As long as some light can penetrate beneath the canopy of leaves (trimming off lower branches will help), an enormous range of plants can be used. There can be flowers all the way from winter with snowdrops (*Galanthus*)

and winter aconites (*Eranthis*), through the spring with bloodroot (*Sanguinaria canadensis*), either in its single or double form, and dicentras, and then on into the summer with various lovely geraniums and meconopsis. Finally the summer ends with drifts of *Cyclamen hederifolium* and then back into winter again with *Cyclamen coum* and *Vinca difformis* providing interest and color. Foliage, in particular hostas and ferns of all kinds, adds a background and interest from spring right throughout the summer months and into the fall. As already mentioned, stick with plants that grow naturally in shady places, rather than trying to force sun-loving plants into what, for them, is really a rather hostile environment.

Plan the bed as you would any other bed, grouping plants of the same kind together, rather than dotting them around. Small drifts, again, would be ideal. Plants do not have to be planted tightly together in a woodland setting, as frequently areas of bare earth are to be found between the drifts. Planting close together obviously helps from the maintenance point of view in that the weeds have less chance to establish themselves, but a more relaxed approach is more in keeping with the setting.

Far left: A natural-looking drift planting of pretty primroses (*Primula vulgaris*), blue *Chionodoxa luciliae* and white wood anemones (*Anemone nemorosa*). This type of planting is ideal under deciduous trees and shrubs which will be covered by foliage later in the season.

PLANTING UNDER TREES

Planting shade-loving plants under established trees is difficult at best and almost completely impossible under conifers. Building the soil up to make raised beds is not a good solution under many plants, as this keeps air away from the surface roots and eventually could kill the tree. A good short-term answer is to plunge large nursery pots in amongst the root spaces. The pots may then be filled with good soil and planted with shade-loving plants. The plastic pots keep the tree roots from invading the good soil. It is a lot of work as it involves carefully hand-digging the holes and it's best undertaken during the winter months when the tree isn't actively growing.

Right: Although bracken (*Pteridium aquilinum*) can be a nuisance in a small garden, it is certainly attractive as the leaves are not only feathery, but also slightly shiny, picking up any available light and reflecting it.

Below: Ostrich ferns, *Matteuccia struthiopteris,* form a perfect light green background against which the blue meconopsis and pink *Primula japonica* are displayed to their best.

DESIGNING WITH GREEN

While the shade gardener has got as wide a palette of colors as any other gardener, the range of plants that supply them are limited. There are only a handful of red-flowered plants, for example, suitable for shade. The most frequent color in shade planting is green, which is represented mainly by foliage. This may seem restricting, but some of the best shade designs are entirely green and it is worth remembering the sheer number of different greens. The interplay of light and dark greens can be enhanced by the play of light across plants.

Similarly, remember that the color varies according to the texture. Shiny leaves are important in dark areas where they pick up and reflect what little light there is. The shape of the foliage also has great effect on the appearance: ferns are feathery and light, for example.

PLANTS SUITABLE FOR WOODLAND BEDS

Achlys triphylla	Iris foetidissima
Actaea	Kirengeshoma
Anemone nemorosa	Lamium galeobdolon
Aristolochia	Lilium martagon
Arum italicum	Lonicera pileata
Asarum	Meconopsis
Brunnera macrophylla	Milium effusum 'Aureum'
Campanula latifolia	Myosotis sylvatica
Cardamine	Omphalodes
Carex pendula	Oxalis acetosella
Convallaria majalis	Pachysandra
Cornus canadensis	Paris
Cyclamen coum	Phlox divaricata
Cyclamen hederifolium	Phlox stolonifera
Daphne mezereum	Polygonatum
Dicentra	Polystichum setiferum
Disporum	Primula
Dryopteris filix-mas	Pulmonaria
Epimedium	Rubus tricolor
Eranthis hyemalis	Ruscus aculeatus
Euonymus japonicus	Sanguinaria canadensis
Euphorbia amygdaloides robbiae	Skimmia japonica
Galanthus	Smyrnium perfoliatum
Geranium	Stylophorum
Glaucidium palmatum	Symphytum grandiflorum
Hedera helix	Tellima grandiflora
Helleborus	Trachystemon orientalis
Hosta	Trillium
Houttuynia cordata	Vancouveria
	Vinca
	Waldsteinia ternata

Above: A well-designed scheme in open shade, demonstrating the wide range of flower and foliage color that can be used in such a situation. *Corydalis flexuosa* provides a clear blue which contrasts with Bowles' golden grass (*Milium effusum* 'Aureum') and rich red dicentras.

OPEN SHADE

Borders that are shaded by buildings, walls or fences can be treated in the same way as woodland areas or can be looked at more in the way that other borders in the open garden are considered. Such positions usually have the advantage that there is no competition from tree roots and therefore all the moisture and nutrients in the beds are available to the plants. The big disadvantage is that plants will often lean forward to get to the light, or worst still are blown forward by the action of the wind rebounding from the wall. Plants, then, as long as they are kept watered, will grow lush in these situations, but may need good supports to keep them in an upright position.

Shrubby plants placed towards the back are not only more resistant to the wind but also filter it, protecting their less strong neighbors. Certainly in such borders the taller plants should be towards the back as in traditional border design, but it may well be beneficial not to have plants too tall in the first place; if you want greenery at the back, use climbers instead. As a matter of aesthetics it is not always a good idea to put all your tall plants at the back, the short at the front and the middlings in the middle. Although this is what one is usually taught, it does tend to create a border that looks like choir stalls. Stick to the general principle, but pull a few of the taller plants forward and allow the heights to vary throughout the border. You will be surprised how much more interesting it will be. Japanese anemones (*Anemone* x *hybrida*), for example, are short in leaf but then throw up taller flowering stems. These can be planted toward the front of a border as the wiry stems do not form a solid mass of foliage, blocking plants behind.

GROUND COVER IN SHADE

Of course not everybody wants to use areas under trees and shrubs as woodland borders. In many cases, it just happens to be part of the garden and they feel they are lumbered with it. All they want to do is as little as possible, but at the same time keep it reasonably neat. In other words, all they are really interested in is in using plants as ground cover. For those without woodland, the type of area that might require ground cover may well manifest itself alongside a row of shrubs along a drive or even underneath an ugly hedge.

There are several plants that can be used as a ground cover. Ivy (*Hedera helix*) is one of the best. Once it has spread across the floor, nothing more need be done. However, if you want to keep it looking at its best then sheer it over every spring and remove any pieces that are attempting to climb up into the trees or shrubs. Lesser periwinkle, *Vinca minor*, can be used in the same way. In lighter shade, perennials can be used. A drift of hostas or shiny bergenias makes a very effective cover as does lady's mantle (*Alchemilla mollis*). Also, *Geranium macrorrhizum* creates a very dense cover of leaves (which have the added bonus of being fragrant) and produces masses of pale pink, pink or purple flowers in early summer, even in quite dark and dry conditions. *Cornus canadensis* is a shrub with an herbaceous habit and quickly spreads to make an effective, dense ground cover, illuminated by its white bracts. Light, which is this time reflected from its glossy leaves, is one of the attractions of using another good ground cover plant, *Pachysandra terminalis*.

Before planting any ground cover, make certain that all perennial weeds have been removed from the area. After planting, mulch well as it will take a while for the plants to spread and completely cover the ground. Most ground cover plants benefit from a sheering to keep them tidy. Ground cover has a habit of trapping any rubbish blowing past, so have a clear up now and again if you want the area to remain neat and tidy.

GROUND COVER PLANTS FOR SHADE

Alchemilla mollis

Bergenia

Convallaria majalis

Cornus canadensis

Epimedium

Erica

Euonymus fortunei

Euphorbia amygdaloides robbiae

Geranium macrorrhizum

Gunnera manicata

Hedera helix

Hosta

Hypericum calycinum

Pachysandra terminalis

Pulmonaria

Stephanandra incisa 'Crispa'

Symphytum

Tellima grandiflora

Tiarella

Tolmiea menziesii

Vancouveria

Vinca minor

Right: As ground cover for shade, few plants surpass *Geranium macrorrhizum*. It not only produces a dense cover of fragrant leaves but also flowers extremely well even in quite dense and dry shade areas.

Far right: Epimediums have attractive heart-shaped leaves and make excellent ground cover for dry shade. Cut back the old growth in early spring to make way for the new.

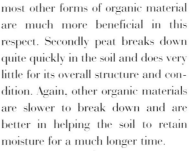

PEAT BEDS

Peat beds are a special form of bed specifically for growing woodland plants. They are the equivalent of the rock garden, but for shade-loving plants. In the past such beds were constructed of peat, hence their name, but nowadays other organic material is used. There are three good reasons for the change to other materials. Peat, although in theory a renewable source, in fact takes far too long to form to be considered as such. In the wild, peat formations support a unique form of wildlife, both flora and fauna, and with large-scale use these habitats are fast disappearing. From a gardening point of view also, there are reasons against peat. Firstly it is a rather sterile medium that adds very little to the soil in the way of nutrients;

most other forms of organic material are much more beneficial in this respect. Secondly peat breaks down quite quickly in the soil and does very little for its overall structure and condition. Again, other organic materials are slower to break down and are better in helping the soil to retain moisture for a much longer time.

As with all beds and borders, careful preparation is the key to success. The most important aspect of this is to be certain to remove all perennial weeds from the site as well as the surrounding area so that they cannot spread back again. Any piece left will come back to be a nuisance later on. Once planted it is virtually impossible to remove this type of weed without dismantling the whole bed and starting again. In lighter soils, digging and removing the weed by hand may be sufficient, but on heavy ones you may have to resort to a herbicide to be certain to remove the lot. Gardeners should be careful of using too many herbicides, but for a once-and-for-all clearance, there should be no lasting problems. Be certain to follow the instructions on the container very carefully indeed.

If possible, leave the ground fallow for several months so that any weeds or parts of weeds that are left reappear and can be removed. Annual weeds are not such a problem, as

their seed will be buried under the layers of the bed, preventing them from germinating.

Peat beds can be constructed on the flat, but they are usually tiered in the same way as a rock garden, with a broad sweep of wide terraces on which to plant. In the past, peat blocks were used to build the low retaining walls of each level. So far no other material has been sold in this form but, for the more adventurous gardener, it should be possible to compress one of the peat substitutes, such as coconut husk fibers, into blocks. They only have to last a relatively short time as the 'walls' are soon held together by plant roots.

The other method is to use logs. These can be thick ones, wide enough to build the wall in one, or thinner ones that need several logs for each wall, one on top of the other, to get the height required. Logs tend to rot after a few years, but again this does not matter as the plants by then will hold everything together. And besides, rotting wood is a natural function in a woodland setting.

The infill should be a mixture of roughly 50 percent good loam and 50 percent well-rotted organic matter. If the loam is on the heavy side, then add some grit or sharp sand to ensure that the drainage is adequate. The idea of a peat bed is that it should

Right: A small peat bed can be constructed using logs to maintain the levels.

1. Dig the ground deeply, adding plenty of organic material. Arrange the first line of logs to mark the edges of the bed.

2. Fill in the space behind the logs with a mixture of good loam and organic material, firming it down and bringing it up to the top of the logs.

3. Add a second layer of logs on top of the soil to form a second tier and back-fill as before.

Left: Peat beds are good for plants that need to have a moist root run, such as *Onoclea sensibilis.* However, it does spread quickly so should be only used in large beds.

Below: A small-scale peat bed with hostas, ferns, ivy and variegated azalea foliage forming a backdrop to *Primula vialii* and dainty campanulas.

retain moisture, but not to the extent that it becomes waterlogged, hence the need for reasonable drainage. The best material is leafmold and all attempts should be made to make as much as possible (see page 29). Composted bark is also excellent, although non-composted bark is not very good, especially if it is in large chips or flakes. Garden compost is very good, as is farmyard manure, although both can be a bit too rich, allowing plants to become too lush and out of character. It is the fibrous quality that one wants, rather than too much in the way of nutrients.

Mark out the bed on the prepared ground. Build up the first wall. It should not be too tall, 10 inches will be more than adequate. Fill in behind, leveling out the bed. If you are building a second layer, build the wall on top of the bed and again fill in with your chosen material. Carry on in a similar manner until the bed is complete. Plant and then mulch with a layer of organic material, preferably leafmold. When planting, some plants, primulas for example, can be set in the vertical walls.

Peat beds, because of the nature of the peat, are usually acidic. Most leaf-molds are inclined toward acid, and this can be increased by mixing in a quantity of rotting pine needles. Traditionally this type of bed has been used for growing acid-loving plants and so the smaller rhododendrons and azaleas are frequently seen as well as many other dwarf acid-loving shrubs, such as the phyllodoce and vacciniums.

PLANTS SUITABLE FOR PEAT BEDS

Anemonella thalictroides
Anemonopsis
Arisaema
Cardamine
Cassiope
Clintonia
Cornus canadensis
Corydalis flexuosa
Cyclamen
Daphne mezereum
Dicentra
Disporum
Dodecatheon
Epimedium
Erythronium
Gaultheria
Glaucidium palmatum
Hacquetia epipactis
Helleborus
Heloniopsis
Hosta
Jeffersonia
Kirengeshoma
Omphalodes
Pachysandra
Paris
Phlox divaricata
Phlox stolonifera
Phyllodoce
Polygonum
Primula
Pulmonaria
Rhododendron
Sanguinaria canadensis
Saxifraga fortunei
Scoliopus bigelowii
Tiarella
Tricyrtis
Trillium
Uvularia
Vaccinium
Vancouveria

Above: Most shade-lovers can be grown in pots.

1. Cover the bottom of the pot with a layer of irregular stones, then part-fill with a good potting compost.

2. Settle the plant on the compost, making sure the top of the rootball is an inch below the pot rim.

3. Fill the spaces around the rootball with more compost and firm gently.

4. Water well, soaking the compost.

CONTAINERS IN SHADE

In general gardening terms, containers are mainly thought of as something you use in sunny or at least light parts of the garden. However they can equally be used in shadier areas. While the full range of bedding plants cannot be used, there are a few bright ones that can be used to lighten up a dull corner. Impatiens will supply bright reds, oranges, pinks and whites, with the waxy *Begonia semperflorens* providing a similar cheerful color range. White is a particularly good color for a shady spot as it shows up so well; what was a dull, shady corner can be transformed by a single pot of white impatiens.

The use of containers is not restricted to housing bedding plants. There are many other plants that can be grown in them, indeed, almost any plant can be as long as they are well looked after. Foliage plants, such as hostas and ferns, can look fantastic in containers. Shrubs can also be grown.

One interesting point about containers is that they isolate the plant from the soil below. For example, in chalky areas it is impossible to grow rhododendrons in the open garden. It is possible to dig a hole, put in a plastic membrane and top up with acid soil, but before long this will turn alkaline and any rhododendron you have planted will quickly turn up its toes. On the other hand, acid soil in a container will be perfect for rhododendrons and other ericaceous plants such as pieris or camellias. In other words, containers are the only satisfactory way of growing rhododendrons and their like in areas with chalky or limy soils.

Another advantage of containers is that they can be moved. This allows for a changing display, bringing forward plants that are in flower, while moving out those that have gone over. It allows the plants to be rearranged at will. It also allows tender plants to be grown outside during the summer and moved under shelter for winter protection.

Containers for shady areas should be created and maintained in much the same way as for those in full sun. They can be made of any suitable material and be of any shape as long as they have drainage holes. Partially cover the hole with an irregular stone so that it prevents the compost falling out, but at the same time does not block the passage of water. Fill the pot with a good quality potting compost. The compost can be mixed with some slow-release fertilizer and, if you think it is worthwhile, with water-retaining crystals. These crystals swell on contact with water, holding it until it is required by the plant's roots. Most types claim to reduce the need for watering by a third, but even so pots should still be watered every day. Finally plant up the container with your chosen plants.

Appearance is often improved by top-dressing the container with a layer of grit or small stones. This is not necessary with quick-spreading annuals which will soon cover the bare compost. Top dressing not only improves the look of the container but also helps to keep the weeds down and moisture in.

Always look after containers: water and feed regularly. Deadheading and generally tidying the plants is something that often gets overlooked, but a little attention will keep them always looking at their best.

On the whole, containers look out of place in a woodland setting, but are extremely useful in other shady

contexts. They are particularly welcome in patio or basement gardens where there is a lot of open shade cast by surrounding walls. They can be placed on steps or even on top of low walls. They can be used anywhere where it is not possible to plant because of paving or some other hard surface, or because services, such as drains, pass just under the surface. Containers can also be used as temporary decoration. For example, if you are entertaining, they can be moved to decorate a sitting area. Even pots of sun-loving plants, which are generally brighter in color, can be moved to shady areas for a short while, even up to a couple of days, without spoiling the plants growing in them.

Large containers can be used by themselves, creating a focal point or possibly associating with plants behind them, but grouping containers can be very effective. It allows height and contrast to be created, as well as the ability to move the containers around within the group or to introduce new ones and remove others. In a group you may well keep one or two foliage plants, hostas for example, to form the basic structure while moving in other plants, such as lilies, as they come into flower.

When visiting other gardens, look to see how containers have been used. With imagination they can be used in a way that is attractive and practical.

PLANTS FOR SHADY CONTAINERS

Begonia semperflorens
Buxus sempervirens
Camellia
Chionodoxa
Cyclamen hederifolium
Ferns
Fuchsia
Galanthus
Hedera
Hosta
Impatiens
Lilium
Nicotiana
Primula
Rhododendron
Skimmia
Viola x *wittrockiana*
Zantedeschia

Above: A container which demonstrates the importance of foliage which far outlasts the flowers of the plants. Here, hostas combine with the leaves of violets, epimedium and primulas.

Left: A very colorful display of tobacco plants (*Nicotiana*) and *Begonia semperflorens*, both of which enjoy shade.

Right: Box (*Buxus*) lends itself well to formal shapes and is also happy in a shady place.

SITTING AREAS

Sitting and eating areas in the garden should not just be barren patios, but a space made more interesting and relaxing by the inclusion of plants, either planted directly in the soil or in containers. As a contrast, on an open terrace where the sun is too fierce, a shady canopy of vines can be created by growing them over a framework of poles (see page 43). In larger gardens, a bower or arbor can be created much in the same fashion from either climbing plants or shrubs, or indeed a mixture of both.

In all these cases the object is to produce a relaxing atmosphere and nothing adds more to this than scent. There are several climbing plants that are perfect for this. *Clematis montana* produces its vanilla scent in late spring or early summer, followed by honeysuckle (*Lonicera periclymenum*) and scented roses (*Rosa*) throughout the summer.

Color can be provided by flowers or foliage. Flowering plants can be used over the arbor and can include many of the clematis and roses that do not have scent as well as those that do. It can also include shade-loving plants around the edge of the arbor or shady area. These can be planted in small beds or placed in containers. If the latter are used then sun-loving plants, such as pelargoniums, can be used for brief periods actually within the shade to brighten it up.

As well as the many shades of green there are other attractive foliage colors that can be used. The golden hop, *Humulus lupulus* 'Aureus', will produce a canopy of wonderful gold, but beware as the stems are rough and

Above: Honeysuckle (*Lonicera*) is the perfect climber for a sitting area as it is highly fragrant.

Left: A vine-covered pergola creates a sitting and dining area for hot summer days.

Below: Seats need not be too formal, especially in woodland gardens.

can cause a weal if the skin brushes against it. There are several variegated climbers from which to choose, but one of the best is *Jasminum officinale* 'Aureum'. As well as having gold-splashed leaves, it also has wonderful, sweetly-scented flowers. Most of the productive grape vines tend to be green, but the leaves of *Vitis vinifera* 'Purpurea' have a curious golden tinge to the new leaves before they turn purple and finally take on a gorgeous fall coloring; a plant well worth growing even if its sour grapes do not amount to much.

Of course shade need not be quite so formal. Simply sitting or lying under a tree is a very pleasant way to pass a summer's afternoon. For such, all you need is a patch of grass on which to sit or lie. Perhaps a little more comfortable would be a seat. A white wooden or metal bench has a classic look to it when positioned under a large spreading tree. It makes a wonderful focal point. More complicated and expensive, but having a quality all of its own, is a tree seat, where the seat is circular, built around the trunk. One way of relaxing in shade that always gives the appearance of complete decadence is a hammock slung between low branches or even between two trees. The problem with hammocks is that not much gardening gets done.

FRAGRANT CLIMBERS FOR SITTING AREAS

Actinidia

Akebia

Clematis montana

Clematis rehderiana

Itea ilicifolia

Jasminum

Lathyrus odoratus

Lonicera

Passiflora caeruleum

Rosa

Trachelospermum

Wisteria sinensis

Above right: A stone seat fitting in perfectly in a woodland clearing.

Right: This glade provides an ideal shady setting for complete relaxation. Although this is on a grand scale, a similar effect could be created in a small space.

Far top right: Brunnera macrophylla enjoys dappled shade in a glade around the silver trunk of a birch (*Betula utilis jacquemontii*).

WOODLAND CLEARINGS

If you are lucky enough to have enough space for a wood, even a small wood, then one of the joys is the spaces between the trees, the open bits where the sun breaks through. Being surrounded by trees these spaces are often very secluded and secret. This is just the place for a secret garden. It would be wrong to make this too formal or even to use garden plants. This is the place to use those wild plants that grow locally on the margins of woods. Cultivate the whole space, so that the rank weeds and grasses are removed to be replaced by soft grasses and wild flowers.

Soon you will not be the only visitor; your clearing will be filled with butterflies and birds. The former will happily be attracted to the wild flowers and relative calm of the clearing, while the latter will come to feed on the seeds and insects that live on or among the plants. Planting berried shrubs and climbers will help to attract the birds as well as small mammals. Water, either as a pond or stream, will also help to attract wildlife to the clearing.

It is essential to have some form of seat in the clearing to enjoy its tranquillity as well as the wildlife there. To observe rather than be observed, a seat under the trees or even a hide will allow you to see even more.

Avoid using garden plants in such a setting. The plants in the center of the clearing should be meadow plants that are able to grow among the soft grasses. On the edge of the clearing and under the shrubs and trees at the margin should be those woodland plants that like such conditions. It goes without saying that all plants should be planted in a natural design, perhaps planting a few plants and letting nature spread them by setting seed. It is possible simply to scatter seed yourself rather than planting, but somehow this never seems to work as well as putting out a few established plants and allowing nature to take over.

Once things are established it is essential to cut the grass at least once a year and preferably twice. The first cut should be in midsummer after the spring and early summer flowers have set seed. The second cut should be a month or six weeks later. If the clearing is left to its own devices it will soon disappear. First rank weeds and brambles will appear, followed by birch and then other larger trees. Eventually it will be covered with trees and indistinguishable from the rest of the wood.

Other areas of the wood should also include seating. The most natural form would be logs or tree trunks, but wooden benches are also suitable. Even a few trees at the bottom of a medium-sized garden could contain such seats, possibly where sun breaks through. Seats can also be placed in a secret clearing made in a thicket of shrubs in even quite small gardens. Such areas create an aura of their own, even a fantasy world away from the urban life beyond, and are welcomed by adults and children alike.

and colorful flowers, can look very exotic, and provide interest during the colder months of the year.

Group the plants to screen off the surrounding garden. This works well round a patio, creating a good place for entertaining, especially at night when soft lighting enhances the effect.

INSIDE OUT EXOTICA

A surprising number of house plants can be moved outside in their pots during the summer to add to the picturesque effect. Not only will they often benefit from being in the fresh

A SHADE EXOTIC

In the small town garden, it is possible to go for a more exotic approach to shade. Why not create a rich extravaganza of foliage and exotic flowers that is more approaching a steaming jungle than a scene reminiscent of a peaceful woodland floor?

This is not as difficult as it may seem, even in cold areas, as there are plenty of plants that can be used to create the illusion. Bamboos, for example, can be used for height and for their restless rustling. Large-leaved plants such as the impressive *Paulownia tomentosa* or the divided leaves of the sumach, *Rhus typhina*, all help with the effect. At lower levels, hostas and ferns can provide more lush foliage for the jungle background. Large strap-like leaves, such as those of phormiums,

especially the brightly-colored forms, all add to the scene. Striking variegated grasses can also be used to the same effect.

There are not many hot-colored plants that can be grown in the shade, impatiens and begonias being two exceptions. Use the exotic reds and flame colors to liven up the dominating foliage. Similar-colored lilies can be used to great effect, either planted directly into the ground or in pots. Flame-colored nasturtiums are easy to grow and provide trails of shocking color.

For cooler effects use arum lilies, *Zantedeschia aethiopica*, with their curled white trumpets and glossy arrow-shaped leaves. Often quite common plants, such as camellias, with their glossy dark green leaves

Above: A variety of large, lush leaves gives the impression of a jungle in a small town garden. The huge leaves of *Paulownia* and the long leaves of the banana palms add sheer size, while dark-leaved cannas add a touch of exotic color.

Right: A variegated bamboo (*Arundo donax versicolor*) forms a highlight in front of deep red *Canna* 'Roi Humbert' and the purple foliage of a phormium.

air and rain, but they will certainly add a touch of exotica to the scene. Some can be planted directly into the soil, particularly if they have been specifically grown for the purpose, but there is no reason why the majority should not be left in their pots, so they are ready to move back inside when the fall approaches. Err on the cautious side and do not put them outside until the night time temperatures are well above freezing. Also avoid placing them where they are in a draught; constant wind funneling between two buildings, for example, will do them no good at all. Having said that, many pot plants will transfer safely and happily outside to great effect. Use plants with exotic-colored leaves such as *Cordyline terminalis* with its rich red coloring, or the spider plant, *Chlorophytum comosum* 'Vittatum', with its striped, arching foliage. Trailing plants can be hung in their original containers to produce long swags of lush foliage on the patio. Sweetheart plant, *Philodendron scandens*, or devil's ivy, *Epipremnum aureum*, are two plants that can be used successfully in this way.

INDOOR PLANTS FOR THE EXOTIC SHADY PATIO

Aspidistra elatior (cast-iron plant)

Chlorophytum comosum 'Vittatum' (spider plant)

Cordyline terminalis (tiplant)

Epipremnum aureum (devil's ivy)

Fatsia japonica (false castor-oil plant)

Philodendron scandens (sweetheart plant)

Platycerium bifurcatum (staghorn fern)

Rhapis excelsa (bamboo palm)

Tradescantia spathacea 'Variegata' (boat lily)

Many gardeners have problems with north-facing walls as they are dark, dry and often cold. But as with all aspects of gardening, it is simply a question of firstly growing what would naturally grow in such conditions, rather than trying to impose your will on plants that are totally unsuitable, and secondly trying to improve the conditions.

Taking the conditions first. There is little that can be done with walls that do not receive much light except by painting an opposite wall white, or another light color, to reflect light toward it (see page 46). What can be improved is the dryness of the soil. Dig it deep and add plenty of organic matter. Once planted, keep the border well watered and mulched to help preserve the moisture. The same thing applies to the north side of fences. Shady walls are often north- or east-facing walls which are not only dark, but cold. Fortunately most of the recommended plants for such a situation are hardy and need no extra protection, but in very cold areas, wrapping them with hessian burlap will help keep the frost at bay. Even better protection can be had by packing the space between the hessian burlap and the plant with straw and wrapping plastic sheeting round the outside to keep it dry.

shady walls

Around any building, there is likely to be a wall that is at least partly in the shade, and in all probability one that is completely shaded. This may seem a waste of space from the gardener's point of view, but there is plenty that can be done with it.

There are a number of plants that will tolerate growing on a north wall and will provide not only a good foliage effect but also a display of flowers. Several roses, for example, will grow under these conditions. 'New Dawn' is one of the best and will produce masses of delicately-colored pink flowers under these conditions. It

also is delightfully scented as an added bonus. Parkdirektor Riggers is a vigorous climber with bright red flowers but unfortunately no scent. Both roses constantly flower throughout the summer and into the fall. For the winter and early spring, color can be provided by camellias and rhododendrons, although neither are too keen on frosts.

While most climbing plants in a wild situation will twine or scramble up through other plants, such as trees or shrubs, on the side of a house or against a garden wall, they will need some form of support. For a wall that is not too tall, trellising can be used. This is available in wood or plastic. Most plastic netting that has been specifically designed for the purpose comes with clips that hold it about an inch or so from the wall so that the climber can pass through and up the back, providing it with a hold. For wooden trellising it is necessary to use wooden blocks to act as spacers between it and the wall. If these are not used the trellis is too tight against the wall, preventing the climber from getting a natural grip and making it difficult for the gardener to get string round it to tie in the climber. If the wall is painted it helps to fix the bottom edge of the wooden trellis on hinges with a catch

Far left: While most clematis are happy in sun or shade, they all prefer to have cool roots, with the base of the plant in the shade. Some, such as 'Nelly Moser' shown here, are better in shade as the petals stay vibrant for longer if they are not bleached by the sun.

Right: Camellias, such as 'E.G. Waterhouse', do well in the shade against a north-facing wall.

Far bottom right: Chaenomeles bloom in late winter or spring, then produce attractive, edible fruits later on in the year.

Below: It is essential to tie in climbing plants or they will thrash about in the wind, injuring themselves and passers-by.

1. Loop the string twice around the trellis support.

2. Tie the ends loosely around the stem of the plant. Don't tie too tight or the string will chafe the stem.

3. Trim the ends of the string to create a neat appearance. Alternatively, use proprietary plastic ties.

along the top. This allows the trellis, plus the climber, to be gently eased away when it is time to give the wall some attention without the plant being in the way. Plastic netting can be unclipped.

For taller walls where a large expanse of trellis would look too overpowering, wires fixed horizontally are the best method of support. Vine eyes are fixed into the walls at 4–5 foot intervals and a strong wire is passed through them and firmly fixed at the ends. The wire should be galvanized so that it does not rust. The whole area should have wires set about 18–24 inches apart.

Plant climbing plants and wall plants at least 12 inches away from the base of the wall. This is partly to avoid the foundations of the building which stick out further than the walls, and partly because the area immediately against the wall is always very dry. Dig a hole much larger than the rootball of the plant and dig plenty of well-rotted organic material into it as well as adding some to the soil that has been removed. Plant the plants to the same depth as they were in the containers, except for clematis which should be planted about 3 inches deeper. Replace the soil around the plant, filling the hole, and water thoroughly. Mulch around the plant.

Before planting, place a cane in the hole near to where the rootball will go and angle it toward the trellising or wires on the wall. Once the plant has been planted, tie it to the cane and, if it is already tall enough, tie it to the bottom wires. Some climbers are self-supporting, while others will need tying in to the supports as they grow. Try and spread the main stems out in a fan, rather than allowing them to go straight up in a single, tangled column. This will make a much better display, covering a larger area.

Keep the plants watered during dry weather, and even in wet weather it is worth checking to see if the rain has reached the soil around the plant as so often a north-facing wall will cast a rain shadow and any plants near it will be starved of moisture. Keep the mulch topped up to help preserve the moisture. At least once a year have a thorough look at the climbers or wall shrubs. Cut out any dead or dying material and tidy up the remainder. Most shrubs and climbers benefit from having up to a third of their old wood removed every year to encourage strong young growth.

DECORATIVE FEATURES

Climbing plants and wall shrubs are not the only way of dealing with shady walls. If you are living in flats or apartments, perhaps the people above you do not want climbers on their walls. Perhaps the area around the wall is paved either with a patio, a yard or just a path—in both cases it will be impossible to plant directly into the ground. It may be that you do not want to cover the walls with climbers as you need access to paint them. Of course you may simply not like climbing plants.

All these reasons add up to thinking out some alternative way of coping with shady walls. The simplest

Above: The simplest and least obtrusive way of supporting climbers on a wall is with horizontal wires. Vine eyes or simple screw-in eyes are positioned at about 4-foot intervals and the wire is threaded through them. The wire is secured by twisting around the eyes at either end.

solution is to hang something on the walls, something that can easily be removed and yet is decorative. The commonest used containers in this situation are window boxes and hanging baskets. There is a lot that can be done with these containers. Some may object that they are rather suburban, but their use is only limited by the gardener's imagination, and if you do not like traditional hanging baskets of petunias and pelargoniums, well sit down and think of something else. Fill them with herbs, for example, or create a ball of cut-and-come lettuces. Use plants that are not commonly seen or use colors and textures in an inventive way. Unlike painting a wall, planting a basket or window box is not a permanent or even semi-permanent thing: you can change your mind whenever you want and replant. You are likely to have to do it every year anyway, leaving scope for new ideas and inventiveness. If you do not like the wire or plastic hanging

baskets that are available from garden centers, why not use willow or redwood baskets, or any other type made from a natural material. They will be more expensive, unless you can find some old ones, but they will also be more attractive.

Of the traditional bedding plants used in window boxes and hanging baskets, impatiens, *Begonia semperflorens*, pansies, and fuchsias are all plants that not only do well in shade but actually prefer it to hot sun. They also all have bright, vivid colors which will enliven a shady spot.

There are a number of different types of pots and other containers that can be attached to walls. Window boxes, for example, need not be attached to windows but can be fixed to a blank wall. Many wall pots are half pots, so that they have a flat side to go against the wall and they frequently have a keyhole at the back so that they can be hung from a nail or hook. All these containers can be filled

PLANTS FOR SHADY WALLS

Akebia quinata

Camellia

Chaenomeles

Clematis 'Marie Boisselot' or 'Nelly Moser'

Euonymus fortunei

Euonymus japonicus

Garrya elliptica

Hedera

Hydrangea anomala petiolaris

Jasminum nudiflorum

Lonicera × tellmanniana

Parthenocissus

Pyracantha

Rosa 'New Dawn' or Parkdirektor Riggers

Schizophragma

BEDDING PLANTS FOR SHADY WALL CONTAINERS

Begonia semperflorens

Fuchsia

Impatiens

Lobelia erinus

Myosotis

Nicotiana alata

Primula

Tropaeolum majus

Viola × wittrockiana

Above: A simple but very effective display for the base of a wall that receives no sun. The contrasts of color and texture are particularly good. Hostas and ferns need little attention other than watering.

hooked tube so that you can water hanging baskets or pots well above head height while comfortably standing on the ground.

Of course, there is no reason why containers should not be placed on the ground at the base of the wall. This gives scope for bigger pots which will be especially good for hostas and shrubs. It also presents the opportunity of building up a larger picture rather than just having a few plants spotted around on a wall.

Wall decoration need not be exclusively confined to plants. There are many other ways of decorating, some temporary and others more permanent. Temporary decorations, perhaps when you are entertaining, might be bunches of flowers, garlands or simply sprays of foliage.

Permanent decoration might well include mosaics. Bright, colored pieces of tile and china can be used to brighten up a dull wall. Pieces of mirror and glass add glitter and sparkle to the design and are perfect for a shady wall. Further sparkle can be created by adding a water spout or fountain to the wall. A wide variety of designs is available from garden centers and specialist nurseries and most of these can be easily installed by the amateur. The sound and sight of moving water can create a tranquil atmosphere and, again, it is perfect for a shady position. However, do consider the wall on which it is installed. Water can trickle down or splash back onto the wall and if it is an old one it may penetrate to the detriment of the decoration inside the house. Check this out before installing a fountain.

with the same bedding plants as hanging baskets, or you can be more adventurous. Even hostas can be grown successfully in these containers. The variegated forms, especially those with white or yellow markings, look especially good on a shady wall.

Using plant containers on walls is not without its problems. Any water that pours through the container can leave a stain on the wall. This may not show on a plain brick wall but it may

be unsightly on a painted one. Another problem with older house walls is that if there is not a cavity in the wall, water from the container may seep right through, leaving a damp patch on the inside of the house. A different problem, but a serious one for some, is that plants need to be watered, and a watering can can be very heavy. It is possible to buy special pump-action watering devices which deliver water from a container up through a long,

GLORIOUS TRUMPETS

Campsis *x* tagliabuana 'Madame Galen' (left) is a superb flowering vine which blooms in late summer when many other climbers have gone to seed. It is perfect for adding interest to a plain wall, especially a white one, against which the flowers will really show. All campsis are prone to sending out unwanted suckers. When planting, dig a hole large enough to accommodate a cement sewer tile 3 feet in diameter, burying it so that the rim is slightly higher than the soil surface. Fill it with good soil and plant the vine in the top to keep it contained and happy.

Above: A brick fountain forms a decorative feature on a wall. The pot of hostas is ideally placed to benefit from the humid air around the water.

Left: A colorful display that transforms a plain wall in shade. The blue paint and the pool add an exotic feel, while the plants add color and freshness. The mirrors provide even more color, reflecting the bright plants out in the sun.

Mirrors have already been discussed with regard to reflecting light (see page 46), but they can also be used on a shady wall merely to add more life. A mirror will reflect other parts of the garden, making it look larger as well as adding interesting perspectives and vistas. If the edges of the mirror are disguised it can look like a window through to another area, making it seem large.

Another way of adding interest to a dull, shady wall is by fixing objects to it. These may be wall plaques or other items. There are a large number of *objets trouvés* that can be used, such as pieces of wood, curious pieces of metal, old tools: the only limit is your imagination. Try cementing old bottle bases between the bricks in a wall, rather like colored port holes.

Winter is always an awkward time in the garden. Many gardeners simply pack up shop in the fall and hibernate until the spring bulbs start pushing up through the soil. Fair enough if you really do not like this time of year, but there is still a lot to be enjoyed and anyone who is prepared to go outside will find plenty of interest waiting for them there.

On a more general gardening note, the winter is a good time for working in the garden. If the weather is not too inclement and the soil not too wet or frozen solid, a great deal can be done. Any work carried out on the borders will be repaid by a saving of at least twice that time later in the year. Without any of the herbaceous plants around, it is possible to get onto the beds and thoroughly weed them, dig them over and add a top dressing. Later in the year, once the soil has warmed up, weeds will be growing so fast that it will be difficult to keep on top of them, but if they have already been removed at their infant stage and the soil has been mulched to prevent further germination, a great deal of time will be saved.

In the winter there is a surprising number of plants either in flower, or of interest because of the color of their bark. Trees and shrubs are also very attractive in outline and silhouette at

through the seasons

It is all too easy to make the seasons look the same with the overuse of evergreens, but there is the possibility of much more variation than this in the shade garden. A little careful planning will provide a constant change of scene.

this time of year. The branches of any tree etched against the dying light of a sunny winter's day can be a breathtaking sight, often more so than when the tree is flower. One of the advantages of this sort of pleasure is that it can be appreciated from the warmth of the inside of a house, simply by looking out of the window.

Most of the shade-loving plants that flower in the winter do so under deciduous trees. In other words they are not in shade when they flower, but are in shade later in the year when their covering trees have burst into full leaf.

Quite a large number of winter-flowering plants are strongly scented. Presumably this is because pollinating insects are few and far between at this time of year and the plants need to attract as many as possible. Most of the shrubs are highly scented. *Viburnum farreri* and *V.* x *bodnantense* and their cultivars and hybrids have little bunches of pink flowers which appear in midwinter in many areas and go on well into spring. These are highly scented. Early in the new year, various species of the Christmas box, *Sarcococca*, begin to bloom. These plants have flowers that are rather insignificant from a visual point of view but produce a very powerful and sweet scent that wafts over great distances. A few cut sprigs will fill the whole house with their perfume.

After the sarcococcas come the witch hazels, *Hamamelis* and *Corylopsis*, both with yellow flowers and a curious sharp scent that is quite astringent. The little flowers clothe the naked branches and show up

Far left: The curious strap-like flowers of *Hamamelis* x *intermedia* 'Jelena' are useful for brightening up the gloomy winter days.

Above: The stunning *Rubus cockburnianus.* Cut down the stems each spring to produce new stems for the following winter.

Right: Hellebores are one of the glories of winter. They are available in a range of subtle colors.

Far right: Berries remain on *Skimmia japonica* through winter as they are not favored by birds.

brilliantly in the shafts of sunlight that catch them. *Cornus mas* also has masses of yellow flowers before its leaves appear and these again have a astringent but delightful scent.

What comes as a surprise to many is that there is a winter honeysuckle, or at least several winter honeysuckles. These are shrubs rather than climbers and have pretty, small pale yellow flowers that appear over a very long period from early winter well into the spring. They are sweetly scented with a wonderful heady fragrance and, on a warm winter or spring day, will perfume the garden around them. *Lonicera fragrantissima, L.* x *purpusii,* and *L. standishii* are the three, the former being the most widely available, but there is not a great deal to chose between them; they are all well worth growing.

At ground level there is also plenty to see. The first of the hellebores makes an appearance just before Christmas and they are still in flower as winter turns to spring. They like a deep humus soil. Bulbs start to appear soon after Christmas, with even a few early varieties of snowdrops coming before the end of the old year. However the main flush of snowdrops, *Galanthus,* appears from

February onward. Also about that time of year, the first yellow flowers of the winter aconites, *Eranthis hyemalis*, push their way up through the soil. Their cup-shaped flowers are surrounded by jolly green ruffs. As winter merges into spring, there are plenty more bulbs and other plants to carry the season forward.

Winter-flowering plants are best planted toward the backs of borders where they will show up during winter when nothing else is above ground or is leafless, but will be covered for the rest of the year when other plants take over. Plant one of the fragrant shrubs near the house or close to the front path so that its perfume can be enjoyed every time you step out of the door, even if you are only walking to the garage.

Bark and evergreen foliage probably can be appreciated more during the winter than any other time of year. Plants such as the hollies (*Ilex*) and skimmias not only have shiny leaves which light up dull corners but also

provide colorful berries to enhance the scene. The white trunks of the various birches (*Betula*) and colorful barks of some of the maples (*Acer*) make them great trees for the winter garden. Several of the ornamental brambles, such as the stunning *Rubus cockburnianus*, have white mealy stems, while the willows (*Salix*) provide a range of different colors, including yellow, red and black. To get the best out of shrubs with colored stems, they should be cut to the ground in spring, so that there is plenty of new growth by the following winter. It is these new stems that provide the best colors.

For those restricted to containers, winter pansies are a wonderful standby, providing color throughout the season. There are plenty of other plants to consider, including the winter-flowering heathers, *Erica*, and small shrubs such as *Skimmia japonica* 'Rubella'. In recent times ornamental cabbages have become very popular for providing winter color.

WINTER-FLOWERING SHRUBS

Camellia

*Cornus mas**

*Corylopsis**

Corylus avellana

*Daphne mezereum**

*Hamamelis**

Jasminum nudiflorum

*Lonicera fragrantissima**

*Lonicera × purpusii**

*Lonicera standishii**

*Mahonia**

*Viburnum × bodnantense**

*Viburnum farreri**

*Viburnum tinus**

Vinca difformis

* denotes scented flowers

SOME COLORFUL BARKS

Acer capillipes

Acer griseum

Acer pensylvanicum

Betula ermanii

Betula utilis jacquemontii

Cornus alba 'Elegantissima'

Cornus alba 'Sibirica'

Cornus stolonifera 'Flaviramea'

Corylus avellana 'Contorta'

Eucalyptus

Euonymus alatus

Pittosporum tenuifolium

Prunus serrula

Rubus biflorus

Rubus cockburnianus

Rubus thibetanus

Salix alba vitellina 'Britzensis'

Salix fargesii

Salix purpurea

SPRING

Spring is one of the most delightful times in the garden and it is the one time of year when there does not seem to be any differentiation between the shade and the open border in terms of what will grow in it; plants seem to be popping up everywhere. And what a colorful season it is, with flowers in vivid yellows, red and blues as well as many shades in between. Not only is everything burgeoning in the garden, but gardeners also feel the sap rising and the urge to get out there and do some gardening.

The period between the winter and spring varies in its timing, depending on the weather; sometimes it seems early and at others late. The flowers span the transition, often not so dependent on the weather but on the amount of light and the lengthening days. Thus daffodils may appear from under snow or in glorious sunshine. There are plenty of bulbs around beside the daffodils: snowdrops are still in evidence, while the crocuses are opening where they can catch the sun through the still bare branches. Puschkinias and scillas are creating patches of blue and later in the spring bluebells (*Hyacinthoides*) will make great patches of the same

Above: Spring would not be spring without drifts of daffodils, seen here with *Scilla bithynica*. Both can be grown successfully in open or partial shade.

Below: Three enchanting spring flowers that can be used in containers or in the open ground. Yellow primroses, purple crocuses and 'Tête-à-Tête' daffodils fill a window box.

Below right: A delightful mixture of primroses, lesser celandine (*Ranunculus ficaria*) and *Anemone blanda* growing under shrubs.

color. The native English bluebell, *H. non-scripta*, has elegant, bright blue flowers whereas the Spanish bluebell (*H. hispanica*) which is seen more frequently in gardens, has a much heavier spike, with the colors a bit more on the muted side, and includes pink forms. It has got the advantage, however, as it does not spread quite so vigorously as its English counterpart. While bluebells are a wonderful bulb to grow under deciduous shrubs, caution should be taken in a small garden as they can be invasive and will crop up all over the garden, often in the middle of other plants, making them difficult to extract.

Although there are plenty of flowers about as winter turns to spring, most of the deciduous trees and shrubs seem still to be fully asleep, although the leaf buds on one or two are just beginning to swell. By the time bluebells carpet the floor, the buds are beginning to open and the branches of the shrubs and trees are beginning to turn into a haze of fresh green. As the bluebells fade, many of the woody plants are now in full leaf and the true shady season has begun.

Many plants take advantage of the brief time at the beginning of spring when the weather is warm enough for growth, but the trees and shrubs have not yet put out their protecting veil and so sunlight and rain reaches right down to the ground. A burst of activity takes place when bulbs such as bluebells briefly appear, flower, set seed and then die. Wood anemones, such as *Anemone nemorosa*, *A. blanda* and *A. ranunculoides*, put up their cheerful nodding flowers, that open wide in the sunshine, above their

PLANTS FOR SPRING SHADE

Anemone

Caltha

Camellia

Cardamine

Chionodoxa

Crocus

Daphne

Erythronium

Garrya

Glaucidium

Hacquetia epipactis

Helleborus

Hyacinthoides

Lunaria annua

Lunaria rediviva

Myosotis

Oxalis acetosella

Primula

Pulmonaria

Ranunculus ficaria

Rhododendron

Sanguinaria canadensis

Silene dioica

Above: Rhododendrons and azaleas provide colorful flowers for spring shade. They must, however, have acid soil.

Right: A pergola with pots of magnificent 'White Triumphator' tulips spaced along its length.

Top right: The long tassels and silvery leaves of *Garrya elliptica* make a fine show in spring.

finely-cut foliage. They bloom and then disappear back below ground before the leaves appear on the trees above. The dainty wood sorrel, *Oxalis acetosella*, also carpets the woodland floor in small drifts.

A number of other plants bloom early before the leaves come on the trees, but do not die back entirely, their leaves remaining all year, or at least until later in the year. Perhaps the best loved of these is the dainty primrose (*Primula vulgaris*). This will often start sending up the odd flower around Christmas time, but the main flush of bloom does not get under way until the spring. These like a dappled shade and do not do particularly well in the open unless the soil is moist. Closely allied are the cowslips, which appear much later, but these are essentially plants of open meadows, although they will grow and flower in light shade. Polyanthus have been popular in gardens for centuries and quite rightly so. They are available in a cheerful range of colors and can be used either in containers or in the garden. Although often used as bedding plants in full sunshine, they also do well in dappled shade and there have been several famous "nutwalks" where areas under hazel trees have been carpeted with polyanthus, creating a wonderful tapestry of both bright and muted colors.

Another well-loved spring plant is lily-of-the-valley (*Convallaria*). Given the right conditions of plenty of leaf-mold, its roots will quickly run through the soil to form a large mat of green leaves, with spikes of white nodding flowers popping up among them. Each flower hangs like a stubby bell, filling the air with its enchanting characteristic scent. They may take a couple of years before they settle down, so do not despair if they do not appear to be thriving when you first plant them.

One white-flowered plant that many gardeners would not want to be without is the bloodroot, *Sanguinaria canadensis*. The single form has poise and charm and is often flushed with a mauvish-pink. However, it is the double one that causes a sensation. The flowers form a golf-ball-sized sphere of narrow petals that are glistening white, with each ball sheathed in a curved glaucous leaf, just like a little posy. This is a gem that grows well in cool woodland soil.

As the spring proceeds, several annuals and biennials contribute color to the scene. Fortunately many of these self-sow and so the gardener has very little to do except appreciate them. One of the earliest is honesty, *Lunaria annua*, which has purply-mauve or white flowers. There are also variegated forms. Once the flowers are over, the large silvery seed pods brighten up the shade until they are eventually blown to pieces in the fall. Forget-me-nots (*Myosotis*) produce drifts of pale blue that can be

breathtaking, and all for no effort on the gardener's part. As spring turns toward summer, foxgloves (*Digitalis purpurea*) begin to throw up their tall spikes of purple flowers in the lighter areas of the shady garden.

Many woodland shrubs also flower in the spring. Rhododendrons and camellias are two firm favorites among many. Unfortunately these will only grow in acid conditions and are denied to those who live on chalk unless they grow them in containers, isolated from the alkaline soil.

By late spring, the leaf cover is complete and the area under shrubs and trees becomes sheltered by dappled shade, obscuring many flowers that grow there. However, in most gardens, late spring is characterized by the dazzling or muted colors of tulips. These are essentially plants for an open position but they can be grown in open shade and among shrubs. In Holland, that country most noted for growing tulips, they are often grown in great swathes under high canopy trees.

Above: Hostas provide a good display of foliage from early summer right through into the fall. This *Hosta sieboldiana elegans* has been enlivened with bright orange Welsh poppies (*Meconopsis*) and red primulas.

Above right: Trilliums span the period between late spring and early summer and are some of the more interesting plants for the shade garden. This is the fragrant *Trillium luteum.*

Right: While they will grow in sun, pansies are happier in light or open shade.

SUMMER

The transition from spring to summer is very blurred and it is impossible to say whether some plants truly belong to spring or summer. Not that it really matters as the classification is artificial anyway. The thing to do is simply to grow the plants and enjoy them whenever they flower.

By now the shade under deciduous trees is beginning to deepen. The leaves have spread to all the branches. Some leaves are still a lighter shade of green, reflecting a bit of light to the ground, but as the season wears on, the color deepens and with it the depth of shade. Although perhaps not so well defined as in the spring, there are large numbers of plants that can be grown, both in dappled shade and in particular in open shade against walls of houses and other buildings.

The blue or Himalayan poppies (*Meconopsis*) are something that most gardeners yearn to grow. They can also be some of the most difficult. To be certain of being successful with them, you really need to provide cool, moist woodland conditions. They will not grow well if the ground and atmosphere are dry. If you can provide what they want, however, they are some of the most delightful of plants. The Welsh poppy, *Meconopsis cambrica*, is much easier, perhaps too easy as it does self-sow rather vigorously. It is not the wonderful blue of its relatives, but a rich yellow or orange. This may seem a disadvantage but in fact to see the bright yellow flowers illuminating a gloomy spot can be quite exhilarating. They shine out from under trees and brighten up open shade against north-facing walls with the same brilliance. They are more or less happy to grow anywhere, which cannot be said of the blue meconopsis.

One plant that it is impossible not to enjoy is the trillium. These are delightful plants, with many different species now being grown in gardens. Still one of the great favorites is the wake robin, *Trillium grandiflorum*, especially its double form 'Flore Pleno'. This group of plants is well worth exploring.

There are a limited number of annuals, or tender perennials which are usually treated as annuals, that will grow in dappled shade and open shade. Some of these have already been mentioned elsewhere in the book. Impatiens is one of the best plants to use if you want bright colors. It comes in white, pink, red, orange and purple. It can be grown in a sunny position as long as it is kept moist, but it prefers to grow in light shade and so is ideal for our purpose. It can be used as a bedding plant or in containers of some sort, window boxes or hanging baskets on a north-facing wall for, example. Pansies (*Viola* x *wittrockiana*), fuchsias and begonias also prefer a cool position. Tobacco plants, *Nicotiana*, will also grow in open shade. With the choice of the right plants, summer need not be a dull time in the shade.

As already mentioned, a few roses will grow in open shade and can be usefully employed to cover a north-facing wall. One of the best is undoubtedly 'New Dawn'. This is a delicate pink (which shows up well in murky conditions) and has the advantage of having a good scent. Many climbing and rambling roses can be used to create shade when draped over arbors and pergolas and, of course, many of their flowers will hang down in the shade. In tree and shrub areas, rambling roses will climb right up through the trees to reach the sunlight, giving a wonderful display.

PLANTS FOR WOODLAND SHADE IN SUMMER

Actaea
Ajuga
Aquilegia
Arisaema
Campanula
Cardamine
Cardiocrinum
Cimicifuga
Cornus kousa
Dicentra
Disporum
Ferns
Hosta
Ligularia
Meconopsis
Polygonatum
Rodgersia
Smilacina
Sophora
Stylophorum
Tellima grandiflora
Tiarella
Tolmiea menziesii
Trillium
Uvularia
Veratrum

79

Above: A good mixture of plants growing up and beside a pergola. The white *Rosa multiflora* is scented and thornless, while *Clematis* x *durandii* is an herbaceous plant that dies back each winter. White foxgloves complete the picture.

Right: Many geraniums provide color right through summer. *Geranium psilostemon* will grow in sun or partial shade.

Clematis can be used in the same ways. Many will grow on a wall, some, such as 'Nelly Moser', are best in such situations. They can also be used on pergolas or allowed to scramble up through trees.

There are so many flowering plants that will grow in shade that it is impossible to go through them all here. All are listed in the section on individual plants toward the end of the book, so the gardener can browse through all the possibilities and choose to grow what they like, perhaps varying their choice from year to year.

Foliage is now well up and provides tranquil drifts of greenery across the woodland floor. Hostas are among the leading plants to grow for this effect. There is such a wide range of colored leaves, varying from different shades of green, through golds to blue, as well as variegations in white, silver and gold. The leaves also vary in size and shape, some beginning small and strap-shaped, while others are huge and rounded. Later in the season tall stems of liliaceous flowers appear, more so in lighter conditions. The flowers vary from white, through the palest blue, to blue and then on to violet. What might start out simply as a plant to be used for filling a shady spot could turn out to be something that becomes an obsession, with the gardener eventually collecting hun-

dreds of different varieties. But there are certainly worse plants to collect.

This is the season above all when it is important to remember to keep things watered. Shade under trees and shrubs, in particular, will be very dry as their roots will be sucking up masses of water every day, especially in hot and windy conditions. Weeds, too, will be taking up their share of moisture, so keep them under control as much as possible. Mulching will be a great help, not only in preserving moisture but also in keeping the weeds at bay.

If you are of a tidy mind, remove all the old flower stems and even the complete above-ground parts of the herbaceous and bulbous plants as they die back. In a woodland setting this is not so important as the sight of decaying plants is a natural occurrence, but in open shade beds you may prefer to keep it neat and tidy and remove anything you might consider an eyesore. By removing spent plants, you not only keep the bed in trim but also allow those plants that are still in flower to show up, making a much better display. Do not throw away or burn spent plants, instead compost them and later return them to the soil.

PLANTS SUITABLE FOR OPEN SHADE IN SUMMER

All those from the summer woodland shade list plus:

Acanthus

Aconitum

Alchemilla

Allium

Angelica

Astrantia

Begonia

Bergenia

Clematis

Dactylorhiza

Euphorbia

Fuchsia

Geranium

Heuchera

Impatiens

Macleaya

Nectaroscordum

Nicotiana

Orchis

Persicaria

Rosa 'New Dawn'

Viola

Above: Autumn is a glorious month in the shade garden, with foliage coming into its own, both on and under the trees.

Right: Hardy orchids, like this *Dactylorhiza x grandis*, are among the most attractive of summer shade plants.

FALL

Fall is not a particularly good time for flowers under trees and shrubs, as everything is beginning to look a bit tired. However, it is the season when foliage and fruits come into their own. Trees and shrubs, in particular, often take on wonderful tinted hues, while many are covered with berries or other fruits. Even at ground level, herbaceous plants are starting to change their color as they die back. Many gardeners like to leave dying stems on the plants as they not only give color and texture in the garden, but also provide birds and mammals with seeds and insects throughout the winter months.

Above: For larger gardens, beech trees (*Fagus sylvatica*) produce some of the best fall foliage. On young trees and hedges, the brown foliage is retained throughout winter.

yellow flowers, blackish stems and wide, lobed leaves. It grows best in typical moist, woodland soil.

Needless to say the geraniums still have a few species in bloom and the late-flowering *G. procurrens* is a great one for scrambling up through bushes with masses of pinkish-purple flowers with dark centers. It can get a bit out of control when well-suited, but it is a marvelous plant for a shrubby area.

Blue is not a typical fall color and so the flowers of the willow gentian, *Gentiana asclepiadea*, are most welcome. Another shade-loving plant with blue flowers, although tending more toward purple, is the lilyturf, *Liriope muscari*. It has not only the benefit of its color and late flowering, but also that it will tolerate dry shade.

Bulbs come back into their own during fall. During the summer months, lilies will have put on a good show in shady spots and containers, but now it is the turn of the small hardy cyclamen. *C. hederifolium* is the first to flower followed later by *C. coum*. The former is a great plant for shade, even dry shade. You only need to put in one or two plants and soon new plants will start popping up all over the place. The seed is covered with a sugary substance that is much loved by ants, which carry them off. They eat the sugar coating and leave the seed to germinate, often some distance from the plant. Whole colonies come into being with the ground covered in their pink or white flowers. Leaves appear late but last through winter and well into spring. These are not only attractive (they are often mottled with silver markings) but also act as an effective ground cover.

In open shade, Japanese anemones (*Anemone* x *hybrida* and *A. hupehensis*) are usually still flowering, their white or pink flowers showing up well in the shade. Some astilbes are still producing their spires of white and pink well into fall. These prefer the shade, except when they are in a moist soil. The toad lilies, *Tricyrtis*, with their curious spotted flowers, are also still flowering. Both these and the anemones like a cool, moist soil, with the toad lilies able to take a little more shade than the anemones.

A rather fine flowering plant for the early fall that likes a bit of shade is *Kirengeshoma palmata*. Its attractiveness is due to the combination of clear

Above: The autumn crocus is, in fact, a colchicum, in this case *Colchicum speciosum.* The naked flower stems emerge in fall, with the leaves following in spring.

Above right: Berries and fruits contribute a great deal of color and interest to the fall scene. Many spindles have double value by having colorful fall foliage as well as attractive fruits. This one is *Euonymus europaeus* 'Red Cascade'.

Another fall bulb that can be grown in light or open shade is the autumn crocus. In spite of its name it is not a crocus but a colchicum. The flowers appear in fall without any sign of the leaves, which finally come up in spring.

There are not many shrubs in flower at this time of year. *Osmanthus heterophyllus,* with holly-like leaves, flowers in late fall with scented blooms. It is worth growing, especially in one of its variegated forms.

At the beginning of fall there is still plenty of green foliage around, including that of hostas and ferns. As the season progresses so many of these turn yellow or brown and eventually die back altogether. Some of the ferns, however, remain green throughout the winter. Evergreen trees and shrubs, of course, still retain their green or variegated foliage and thus provide a constant structure to the garden.

A SCHEME FOR ALL SEASONS

The following combination affords enjoyment in every season of the year. Sweet box (Sarcococca confusa) is a beautiful evergreen shrub with dark, shiny green leaves and insignificant, but highly-scented flowers in late fall to early winter. Underplant it with wintergreen (Gaultheria procumbens), a ground-hugging evergreen with white flowers, followed by scarlet fruits in late summer. Add an airy feel to the scene with maidenhair fern (Adiantum pedatum), which unfolds bright green fronds on black shiny stems in spring and maintains its spring-like green all summer long. Last but not least, add variegated Solomon's seal (Polygonatum x hybridum 'Striatum'), which dies back in winter but has three seasons of interest with contrasting foliage, bell-like flowers in late spring and golden fall color.

PLANTS FOR FALL SHADE

Astilbe

Cimicifuga

Colchicum

Cyclamen hederifolium

Eucryphia

Ferns

Gentiana asclepiadea

Geranium procurrens

Hosta

Kirengeshoma palmata

Liriope muscari

Osmanthus heterophyllus

Vinca difformis

FALL FOLIAGE AND BERRIES

Acer

Amelanchier

Berberis+

Betula

Carpinus

Cotinus

Cotoneaster*

Crataegus+

Enkianthus

Euonymus+

Fothergilla

Ilex*

Liquidambar

Malus+

Parrotia persica

Prunus

Rhus typhina

Skimmia*

Sorbus+

Stephandra

* Berried or fruiting trees or shrubs

+ Both foliage color and fruit

Because plants growing in the shade of trees often look as if they are growing in the wild, many people think that they need little or no attention. Like any other part of a garden, if you want to get the best out of it, then it is important to make certain that the conditions are right and the plants are well tended.

The most important aspect of shade management is to ensure that the ground is well prepared in the first place. Unless this has been done, the best will never be achieved and it may even become an uphill struggle to achieve anything at all. Whatever else you do, prepare the ground thoroughly before you begin to plant.

Once the ground is ready and you have planted it up, regular maintenance will help keep it in shape. A little work done often will not only prove easier than having irregular blitzes, but will also save time in the long run. Another way of cutting back on the amount of work to be done is by using a mulch on the soil.

Mulches do several beneficial things. In the first place they should be deep enough to prevent any weed seed in the soil from germinating. Thus they cut down the amount of weeding necessary. In the second they help prevent the loss of moisture through evaporation, which helps to

shade maintenance

No garden will remain a garden unless it is maintained. Even a wild garden needs maintenance, in fact often more so than a conventional garden. The amount of work can be reduced by the use of mulches and by doing a little work often.

reduce the amount of watering necessary. Thirdly, as the mulch starts to break down, it helps condition and feed the ground, leading to another saving in time. Finally, depending on which mulch you use, it can look good, presenting an attractive background against which to see both flowering and foliage plants. So

mulches are very good news for the gardener in many different ways.

There are a number of different materials that make a good mulch (see page 27), and locally there may be others. Before mulching, make certain that the ground has been thoroughly watered, either by rain or by artificial means, such as with a sprinkler. Spread the mulch over the soil aiming, if possible, to make a layer at least 4 inches deep. The mulch needs to be topped up from time to time as it is likely to break down and become incorporated into the soil (which is a good thing). Keep an eye out for areas that have become thin, either because of wind, bird activity, the passage of feet or branches scraping the ground. Top them up as necessary.

Plants do best if they are in a natural environment and there is no doubt if you can create a woodland soil and grow plants that enjoy those conditions then there should be no reason to water. However, gardening never seems to work out exactly as planned and one of the worst variables, of course, is the weather. There are bound to be times when the ground will become too dry and it will become necessary to water.

The only way to do this is to ensure that the soil is thoroughly soaked; it is

Far left: Many plants that are grown in the shade, such as this *Primula pulverulenta*, need moist conditions. One way of preserving moisture is to provide a deep mulch.

CUTTING BACK AND CLEARING UP

Under natural conditions, the flowers of a woodland floor are left to themselves; no one bothers to clear them up. However, in clearings or on the margins where there is more light, the ranker vegetation takes over and eventually it turns to dense woodland, so even in a natural situation some management is necessary if you want things to stay as they are.

In the garden there are other factors at play, one being of course that most of us like to keep the garden looking neat and tidy. Old dead stems, dying plants, even fallen leaves, offend the eye and have to be cleared away. This might not be such a problem in the wilder part of the garden, but where the shade is created by the lee of a house, then any borders here tend to be part of the neater garden.

There are other and possibly better reasons for tidying up the garden. When flowers have been pollinated, the petals die back and the seed begins to swell. The process of forming seed is very expensive in energy

Above: A drip-hose seeps water through its porous surface, keeping the soil moist beneath a mulch.

Right: Helleborus argutifolius is a tough plant which is tolerant of dry, shady conditions and relatively poor soils.

Far right: Once fall frosts have arrived, many plants die back for winter. In cold areas, the dead vegetation protects the dormant plant crown, but hosta leaves turn to mush and are useless for this purpose. They should be removed and composted where possible.

no good just dribbling a little water over the surface. It must be sufficient to penetrate right down into the earth. A watering can is useless except for watering a few individual plants. A sprinkler system is one of the only means to do it. Place a jam jar or rain gauge within the range of the sprinkler so you can get some idea of how much water has been delivered. It should be at least an inch at a time. Dig into the soil to ensure that the water has penetrated, if it has not, continue sprinkling.

An alternative means is to lay a drip-hose just below the surface of the mulch. This device is a porous hose that "sweats" water along its length. When turned on (it is usually left on for a few hours) water dribbles out slowly just keeping the soil moist, without flooding it. Artificial watering sytems should not, however, be used in areas where drought is a common problem.

Woodlands are self-sufficient in nutrients: they do not need artificial fertilizers and you should aim for the same independence in your own garden. In woodlands the rotting leaves return the nutrients to the soil. In the garden, you should do the same by returning leaves, or other materials, once they have broken down.

SUCCESS IN DRY SOIL

Several of the hellebores do well in dry shade, including Helleborus foetidus *and* H. orientalis, *but perhaps the best is* H. argutifolius, *whose clusters of apple green, delicate-looking, yet hardy flowers start to appear as early as February in mild winters. The strong, handsome foliage is evergreen and has spiny edges. It will survive in poor soil under the shade of trees and surrounding shrubs.*

terms, and if the seed is removed, all that energy is available for creating new flowers. So deadheading often promotes more flowering in a plant. It also allows the new flowers to stand out better than if they are surrounded by dead and wilting ones.

For most plants that have a continuation of flowering, it is simply just a question of removing the flower that is going over. Sometimes it may be a whole truss of flowers. Sometimes it is necessary to remove the whole flowering stem. There is no point, for example, in taking off individual flowers from a hosta; it is neater to remove the stem from the base. This is no loss to the plant as there are no leaves on the flower stems. With other plants it is best to sheer off the whole plant at ground level and let it come up again. For example, pulmonarias and *Alchemilla mollis* both benefit from this. Cut them off immediately after flowering and they will put up a flush of new leaves that will look infinitely better than the old ones that you have cut off.

Toward fall, all the herbaceous plants, and many evergreen ones that overwinter as rosettes, die back. In a wild situation these can be left to eventually fall to the ground and to rot, but in a garden situation, as we have already seen, tidiness usually prevails. Some gardeners like to cut these back straight away and have the garden tidy by the onset of winter. The main advantage, apart from making the place look tidy, is that it saves doing it in the spring when there is so much else to do.

However, many gardeners do prefer to leave it until at least the late

winter, if not the spring. One of the main reasons is because many such plants still contain seedheads which provide food for birds and small mammals during the harsh winter months. Insects overwinter in their nooks and crannies, again providing food for birds. Another good reason is that dead stems often have a beauty of their own and add an interesting aspect to the garden during the bleak winter months.

Whenever you do it, do not burn the old stems and leaves. They should all be composted and returned to the soil. If the stems are woody and diffi-

cult to compost, then either break them down by hitting them hard with a hammer or put them through a shredder if you have one.

PROPAGATION: SOWING SEED

One of the easiest ways to increase your stock of shade-loving plants is to grow them from seed. There are, as with all aspects of gardening, advantages and disadvantages.

The big advantage is that you can grow a large number of plants for a relatively small outlay. There is a very large range of seeds available

Above: This technique can be used to sow seeds of most plants.

1. Fill a pot with compost and gently firm down. Scatter the seed thinly over the surface.

2. For fine seed, first cover the compost with a layer of fine grit.

3. Scatter the fine seed over the grit, then water.

4. Cover the coarse seed with sieved compost or with fine grit and water both pots from below by placing them in a bowl or tray of water.

5. Place the pots in a propagator or in plastic bags until germination.

Below: When the seedlings are large enough to handle, prick out into trays of potting compost to give them more space to grow on.

1. Most seedlings are ready to be potted on when the second set of leaves appears. Hold the seedling by a leaf and not by the stem or roots.

2. Carefully remove the seedlings by prising them out of the compost with a pencil. Fill a seed tray with compost and firm gently. Use the pencil to make a small hole in the compost and lower the roots into the hole.

3. Firm the compost gently back around the roots, making sure the seedling is planted to the same depth as before. Water the tray with a fine-rose watering can.

commercially, especially from those seed merchants that specialize in the more unusual plants. Many garden societies run seed exchanges which, in some cases, list several thousand varieties, many of which are not available from any other source. If you are really keen, you can take shares in seed collecting expeditions to remote parts of the world. These are often advertised in specialist gardening magazines. Then of course you can collect seed from your own plants and perhaps swap with friends.

The main disadvantage is that you cannot guarantee how the plant will turn out. When using vegetative propagation, such as taking cuttings or dividing plants, the resulting plants will be identical to the parent. This is not so with seed. The variation might be slight, even unnoticeable in many instances, but nonetheless the plant will contain genes from both the plant from which the seed was collected and its pollinator. The resulting seedling may, therefore, exhibit characteristics of either or both, or even their forebears. Growing hostas, for example, from seed can be a thankless task as the seedlings are often inferior in their foliage markings and other characteristics to their parent or parents. On the other hand you may occasionally strike lucky and get a plant that is infinitely better.

Seed can be sown in the open ground, but it is better done under the more controlled environments of a pot. If you are growing a lot of seed in the hope of getting a good form, then it may be necessary to sow in trays, but for most purposes a 3 or 4 inch pot will produce enough seedlings. Fill the pot with a good seed compost and lightly firm down. Sow the seed thinly on the surface and then cover with a layer of fine grit, a quarter inch deep.

Before you go any further, remember to label the pot. Hosta seedlings, for example, all look the same and you are bound to forget which is which.

The pot of seed can be placed in a heated propagator but most perennials and shrubs do not require any degree of warmth to germinate. Place the pots in an out-of-the-way corner of the garden or outside on a planting bench. If the seeds will germinate better with extra warmth, then grow them in the basement or another warm, convenient spot, preferably out of direct sunlight. Do not let the pots dry out (on the other hand do not keep them running wet). Leave them there until the seed germinates, which in some cases may be a year or more. Do not be in a hurry to throw away ungerminated pots: wait at least three years to see if anything appears.

When the seedlings are big enough to handle, usually once they have their first true leaves (the first pair are the "seed" leaves) they can be pricked out into individual pots and grown on ready for planting out.

VEGETATIVE PROPAGATION

Vegetative propagation, as opposed to seed, takes a piece of the existing plant and turns it into a new plant. For the gardener this mainly means dividing the plant up into two or more pieces, or taking a piece of stem and encouraging it to produce roots and thus a new plant.

The big advantage of this is that you get an identical plant to the parent, so as long as you choose a good form you will have a good plant. But you do need the plant, or at least some plant material in the first place.

Left: Annuals, such as tobacco plants (*Nicotiana*), must be grown anew from seed each year. Plan ahead so the plants are ready when you need them.

Right: Hostas, such as *Hosta fortunei albopicta*, will not come true from seed, so the only way to produce identical plants is to lift and divide clumps.

Below right: Divide hostas when the clump needs to be rejuvenated, or when you want new plants.

1. Dig up the hosta in spring when the shoots are emerging. Use a sharp knife to cut the rootball into smaller pieces.

2. Make sure each piece has a number of new shoots and a good portion of roots.

3. Small divisions should be grown on in pots before planting out. Use a good quality potting compost and keep the roots moist until the plant has recovered.

DIVISION

Divisions are generally best made in fall or spring. Dig up the plant to be divided. A crude method is to insert two garden forks, back to back, in the center of the plant and lever them apart so that the plant divides into two. Repeat until you have the desired number of pieces. A much better method is one that causes far less damage to the divisions and thus provides less chance for diseases to find their way in.

Shake the plant so that the soil falls off, at the same time gently manipulating the roots with your fingers. In many cases the plant will naturally fall into several pieces as the earth falls away. If the soil is heavy or the roots tangled then follow the same procedure except do it in a bucket of water so that the soil washes off. Again for many plants the divisions will just slide apart. For larger and entangled plants, including hostas, once the soil has been washed off look for a bud and with a sharp knife cut that section away from the rest of the plant ensuring that it has plenty of roots attached. For most herbaceous plants, the young growth around the edge of the plant makes the best divisions. The woody center is old growth and should be discarded. Plant the divisions back into the soil or into pots.

CUTTINGS

Most plants can be propagated from cuttings but some plants are more difficult to take than others; and there are some that seem nigh impossible, but with a little experience even these can be conquered.

Cuttings can be grouped in various types but the basic procedure is the same. Part of the plant, usually the stem, is taken and placed in compost until roots begin to form. It is then potted up.

The cuttings can be soft, semi-ripe or hard. Soft ones consist of fresh young spring growth that is still pliable. Semi-ripe cuttings are taken later in the year, around midsummer just when the stem is beginning to harden, so it is not so flexible. Hard-

Above: Geranium endresii self-sows, producing enough seedlings for most uses, but it can be divided to provide even more plants. The shrubby *Cotinus coggygria* should be increased by taking cuttings.

wood cuttings are usually confined to woody subjects such as shrubs and consist of the previous season's growth which has now become hard.

Herbaceous and perennial plants are propagated from soft or semi-ripe cuttings. They in turn can be classified into three groups: basal cuttings, tip cuttings and stem cuttings. Basal cuttings are usually soft growth, taken in the spring just as the shoots emerge from the base of the plant. Tip cuttings are those taken in the summer from the maturing stems, while stem cuttings are those taken from anywhere on the stem.

Cutting material should be free from pests or diseases and should not be a flowering stem. Cut it and pop it into a plastic bag if there is more than

a couple of minutes delay before you can attend to it. If you are taking cuttings from a friend and have to travel before you can plant them, wrap them in moist paper towels or newspaper, and then put them in a plastic bag. Just before potting up, shorten the cutting to about three sets of leaves, cutting through the stem just below the bottom set. Remove the lower two sets of leaves with a sharp knife, leaving just the top set. Dip the base of the cutting into a rooting compound and then insert it into a pot of cutting compost filled with a light planting mixture; 3- or 4-inch pots are a suitable size for most purposes. The planting mixture can be bought from a garden center or can be homemade using 50 percent sharp sand and 50 percent peat or peat substitute. Place up to 12 cuttings round the edge of the pot and then put it in a propagator or cover it with a plastic bag and place on a windowledge out of direct sunshine.

Once the cuttings have rooted (roots will show through the holes in the bottom of the pot) pot them up into individual pots in a regular potting mixture. Harden them off before planting out by gradually introducing them to the conditions outside, a few hours at a time to start with. Do not leave them out overnight until they are fully hardened off.

Hardwood cuttings are taken in late fall or winter, from trees and shrubs. They are inserted straight into the ground in a shady position. After a year, they should have rooted and can be planted out or potted up.

Right: Most shrubby plants are easy to propagate from cuttings, which can be taken in the following way.

1. Prepare the cuttings as soon as you can after taking them from the plant. Trim just beneath a leaf node.

2. Remove the lower leaves with a sharp knife.

3. Fill a pot with cutting compost and make a hole in it with a pencil. Dip the tip of the cutting into hormone rooting powder and insert into the hole. Firm the compost lightly around the cutting.

4. Repeat with the other cuttings, then water. Place the pot in a propagator or plastic bag. When roots appear through the drainage holes, repot the cuttings into individual pots to grow on.

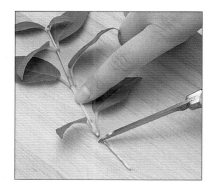

ROOT CUTTINGS

There are a surprising number of plants that can be increased by taking cuttings from the roots. This may seem a strange idea at first, but you only have to remember what happens if you dig up a dandelion or other perennial weed, and miss a piece of the root. Similarly, most gardeners have experienced the problems of leaving only a small fragment of couch grass, bind weed, or ground elder behind and seeing them sprout up new plants in next to no time. Not all plants do this, but many of the thicker-rooted plants, such as brunnera and dicentra, can be increased in this fashion.

One advantage of taking cuttings from the roots is that diseases found in the stems of some plants are not transmitted to the new plants if the cutting is taken from the root rather than the stem. Normally root cuttings are taken when the plant is in a dormant state, which for most plants means in winter. Any time, except when the weather is very cold, will do and many gardeners like to do it in the early winter. To prepare root cuttings, dig up the plant and wash the soil from the roots. Select one or more thick roots that look healthy and have

not been damaged during the process of being dug up. Cut these off and return the plant to the soil.

Cut the roots into 2-inch sections with the cut at the top of the root (that is, the end nearest the crown of the plant) being straight across, and the cut at the bottom being at an angle. This in no way improves the quality of the cutting, it just indicates which is the top and which the bottom.

It is not always necessary to remove the plant from the ground. Careful excavation down one side will often reveal enough roots for cuttings.

Fill a pot with cutting compost and plant several cuttings into it. They should be placed vertically with the flat end at the top. Cover with about half an inch of compost and then top dress with fine grit. An alternative is to arrange the cuttings horizontally in trays of cutting compost and again cover them with compost and a layer of fine grit. The latter method is particularly suited to thinner roots, but the method you choose is up to you. Place the pot or tray into a cold frame, or in a convenient corner outside. Shoots and leaves will begin to appear in spring. Once roots are well established, pot up individually or plant straight out into a border.

Hostas are among the most popular of garden plants, but unlike most of the others at the top of the list, hostas are there mainly because of their foliage. Alas they are herbaceous and die back during the winter, but they are with us for the other three seasons of the year, providing a mixture of excitement and practicalities. The excitement comes from the huge range of different shapes, colors and textures of the leaves and the diverse ways in which these can be used. The practicalities come from the fact that hostas are good 'sensible' plants. They can create a backbone for borders throughout the seasons and are dense enough to provide ground cover in shady areas.

Hostas are not a very big genus as some plants go. There are only about 40 or so species (anywhere between 20 and 50 in fact, depending on who you believe), but on the other hand there are countless thousands of cultivars, most of which have been bred in America or Japan. In the wild they originate from eastern Asia: from China, Japan and Korea. They are basically woodland plants that like to grow in light shade. The marvel of hostas is that they will grow in moist, boggy conditions as well as very dry situations.

The size of hostas varies considerably from tiny plants not more than a few inches high to enormous clumps up to 2 feet tall (or more if you include the flower stems). An individual plant will form a dome of foliage, as it ages so it expands and the dome grows broader. When several hostas are planted near each other the plants merge to form a continuous and effective ground cover.

shady characters

For all the planning and designing, it is the plants themselves that make a garden. There are a surprising number from which to choose, covering a wide range of colors, sizes and seasons. But of all plants, the hosta must remain a leading contender.

Nearly everybody that grows hostas does so for their foliage. The shapes of the leaves vary from thin narrow ones to those which are almost round. The surface is often heavily pleated, creating a play of light and shade. The margins also vary from flat to wavy. Their texture can vary from the shiny to dull.

There is a tremendous variation in color, although the range of colors is relatively limited. As with all foliage the basic ingredient is green, but as anyone who has looked at a display of hostas will know, there is an enormous number of different greens, from light green to dark green. The textures of the leaves, in turn, affect these colors: a shiny dark green is quite different from a dull dark green.

The influence of white and cream and yellow and gold changes the leaves completely, they suddenly become much more alive. The green is never lost (if it was the plant would not be able to photosynthesize and produce food); it is always hovering in the background. In the main the green leaves are either margined with white or yellow or the green itself is the margin and the variegation is in the center. The variegation can be either regular or irregular. The leaves are rarely splashed with irregular splashes.

Far left: The versatility of hostas is demonstrated here by the way this *Hosta crispula* fits perfectly into a green and white scheme with 'Mount Tacoma' tulips.

Sometimes the whole leaf is yellow or gold, but there is always some green in the color, and even if the leaves open up as a pure color, they soon begin to become tinged with green.

The only real color break is that some hosta leaves have a blue coloration, admittedly a greenish blue but blue nonetheless. Although green leaves can also be glaucous (covered with a sort of fine greyish powder) it is most notable on the blue forms. This gives them an added attraction.

Hosta flowers are often overlooked in the enthusiasm for the foliage; indeed some growers even cut them off. However, they are a very attractive part of the plant. The generally leafless stems are thrown up well clear of the foliage, each bearing a series of pendulous, lily-like flowers. The flowers vary from white and lilac right through to quite a dark blue. They do not flower very well in dark conditions, but will do so in light shade. The light coloration of the flowers means that they stand out beautifully when many other flowers fade into the shadowy background. They appear from midsummer onwards.

Hostas are very valuable in the garden. Apart from anything else they simply look good and fit in with so many other plants. On top of this they make valuable, attractive ground cover. One of their most important contributions to the garden, especially as far as this book is concerned, is that they are superb plants for shady conditions, either under trees or in open shade against north walls.

One aspect that is often overlooked is that they grow well in pots and other containers. These can be placed

Above right: A solid line of hostas clearly defining the edge of a border and acting as a neutral foil to *Rosa* x *francofurtana.*

Above far right: The acid green leaves of *Hosta fortunei albopicta aurea* brighten up a dull corner.

in full sun if they are kept well-watered, but are best used in shady areas where it may be difficult to find other subjects for containers. Although clumps can be grown in the border for many years, it is necessary to repot those grown in containers every three or four years to keep them looking fresh and at their best and prevent them becoming too pot bound.

The cultivation of hostas is very straightforward. They do best in a typical moist woodland soil, that is one that includes plenty of well-rotted organic material. If possible treat the whole border but if compost is in short supply, just add it to the area around the plant. They grow best in light shade but can also be grown in full sun, although it is then essential to keep the soil moist (they are more tolerant of drought in shade). Another advantage of light shade is that overhanging trees or shrubs offer some protection from hail. This may seem trivial but in areas prone to summer storms this may be of importance, as the foliage can be shredded in seconds by a sudden downfall. Wind can also be a problem, especially if laden with sea salt. Again shrubs and trees will afford protection, but it may be necessary to provide extra windbreak in extreme conditions.

The best times for planting are in fall, while the soil is still warm enough for the roots to become established, or in the spring as things are warming up. Always plant to the same depth as they were in their pots. After planting, water well and mulch to preserve moisture. Water daily, if necessary, for a week or so until the plant becomes established.

One of the most serious problems for any grower is slugs and snails. These can ruin the appearance of any hosta in a single night. Going out at night with a torch and collecting up any you can find will reduce the population. Slug bait is an option for those who do not mind using chemicals, indeed it is the only sure way of totally protecting the foliage. Various other traditional methods are often recommended, such as surrounding plants with ashes or grit, but these rarely deter the determined slug.

A SLUGPROOF HOSTA

Hosta '*Sum and Substance*' (right) is a real winner in that it can tolerate both sun and shade. The leaves are probably best described as a golden green, though they appear pure gold when seen in full sun. They are enormous — more than 18 inches in length and at least 12 inches wide. The plant forms a marvelous clump of stunning foliage, almost 3 feet high. It produces beautiful lilac flowers on tall stems in summer. If that's not enough to convince you to try it, the tough leathery leaves are totally slugproof, even in the wettest of years.

Other major pests in some areas are voles and moles. They will come up from underneath and pull an entire plant underground. To prevent this from happening, plant hostas with chicken wire or other wire netting around their roots to protect them. Deer also feast on hostas, eating the leaves and leaving bare stems.

The other problem that besets many growers is that a late frost can turn the emerging leaves to mush, from which the plants will not fully recover until the following year. The only solution is to keep an eye out for frosts and cover your hostas with fleece, old blankets, sheets, towels or anything else you have to protect the plants. Growing under trees or shrubs will give some protection and it will only be severe frosts that will be a problem here. General winter protection may be needed in cold areas. Here a covering of straw or bracken or other mulch should be sufficient.

Hostas can be left in the ground for years without attention, but they will become congested and benefit from being lifted, divided and replanted in rejuvenated soil. This is easy to write but it is not a job for anyone who is not fit and should be avoided if you have back problems. The same problem comes if you want to propagate by division; the clumps may be too big to handle. A crude but successful method is to simply chop a slice off the clump with a sharp spade.

The best way to increase hostas is by division, as already discussed (see page 89). Seed can be sown, of course, but they are unlikely to come true (that is, resemble the parents). The best time for dividing is in the spring just as they are coming into growth. If you can lift them, do, and wash off any soil so that you can see the root structure. Choose strong buds with plenty of root attached and sever with a knife from the rest of the clump. Pot up or replant the divisions immediately.

Hostas are extremely hardy and can survive temperatures as low as about −40°F. In fact, they need some chill to grow well, and do best in climate zones 3–8.

Right: A superb specimen of 'Gold Standard' with layer upon layer of leaves creating a perfect mound.

Far right: Hostas make wonderful subjects for tubs. This collection shows a good range of leaf shapes and colors in a varied display.

HOSTA SPECIES

H. CLAUSA

A low-growing species (up to 8 inches high) that spreads extensively by stolons. It has dark green leaves. The flowers never fully open. The species is seldom seen but the variety normalis is commonly grown. This does have flowers that open, to a blue, making it a good low ground cover plant.

H. CRISPULA

A medium-large (up to 16 inches high) species of hosta with deep green leaves with wavy margins irregularly marked in white. The flowers are a pale lavender. It is best planted in shade, out of full sunlight. It is susceptible to wind damage, but that apart, it is a superb plant.

H. DECORATA

A low hosta (up to 10 inches high) with dull green leaves with a wavy, white margin. The flowers are dark violet-blue. It is a stoloniferous, slow-spreading plant. It is not the easiest of hostas to grow, but seems to be increasing in popularity.

H. ELATA

A large hosta (up to 30 inches high) with variable characteristics although generally with matt dark green leaves with undulating margins and prominent veins. It has mauve flowers with yellow anthers.

H. crispula

H. fortunei aurea

H. FORTUNEI

A large species of hosta named after the plant collector Robert Fortune. The identity of the species has a confused past and has now been lost. However, it has left a legacy of good forms that are much grown in the garden. They are not very tall plants, up to about 14 inches high, but they have a wide spread and make good ground cover plants. Their flowers are dark lavender or pale purple. H. f. albopicta has yellow leaves (which turn greener as they age) with green margins. There is a form of this with all-yellow leaves, without the green margins, called aurea. H. f. aureomarginata, as its name suggests, has golden yellow margins to its green leaves.

H. LANCIFOLIA

A small-medium sized hosta (up to 12 inches high) with narrow leaves that are a shiny dark green. The flowers are purple. This is a stoloniferous plant which gently spreads. It is a beautiful species to try.

H. MINOR

As its name implies this is a very small hosta, growing up to only 5 inches in height. The leaves are undulate and are a mid green. The flowers are light purple. (The white-flowered form alba is now generally considered to be a variety of H. sieboldii.) The plants are stoloniferous and spread. A good low-growing hosta for a shady rock garden or a peat bed.

H. MONTANA

A variable species but typically a large hosta (up to 30 inches high) with matt to glossy, dark green leaves. It has off-white to pale mauve flowers. An erect plant that makes a good specimen. One of the best forms is known as 'Aureomarginata'. This has very large glossy green leaves with irregular yellow margins and lavender flowers. A superb plant but slow to establish.

H. NIGRESCENS

A medium to tall hosta (20 inches high) with leathery, dark green leaves that are dusted with grey on their emergence. Near white to pale purple flowers. It is called nigrescens because of its black emerging shoots.

H. fortunei aureomarginata

H. nigrescens

H. PLANTAGINEA

A large hosta up to 24 inches high with heart-shaped leaves of a glossy, yellowish green. The flowers are one of its great features: they are large, waxy and pure white. They open at night and are fragrant. The form japonica (previously known as grandiflora) has larger flowers. It is sometimes known as the August lily.

H. SIEBOLDIANA

This is one of the best-known of all hostas. It is a large plant, up to 30 inches tall, with large waxy, blue-green leaves that have a glaucous bloom. The flowers are a dirty white. It is more tolerant of drought conditions than many other hostas, but is at its best where moisture is available. The variety elegans is even better than the species, with large, puckered leaves and lilac flowers.

H. sieboldiana elegans

H. sieboldiana

H. SIEBOLDII

This is often confused with the previous species because of its similar name, but it is quite different. This is a low plant, only growing to 12 inches, with narrowish, lance-shaped leaves colored a matt dark green and 3–4 pairs of veins. The flowers are striped white and purple. It is a good ground cover plant that tolerates both excess moisture and dry conditions. There are several varieties and cultivars of which kabitan is one of the best. This has bright yellow leaves with a narrow, dark green, undulate margin. Flowers are a rich purple. A striking plant.

H. TARDIFLORA

This is a small hosta (up to 10 inches high). The narrow and lance-shaped foliage is leathery and is a smart, glossy dark green. The flowers are lavender in color and do not open until the fall.

H. TOKUDAMA

A small to medium hosta (up to 12 inches high) which is a smaller version of H. sieboldiana. The rounded leaves are a rich glaucous blue and very puckered, giving it a distinctive look. The flowers are a dirty off-white. This plant is very slow to increase. It has several forms and cultivars of which flavocircinalis is probably one of the most popular. This is a much larger plant with irregular yellow-gold margins to its leaves and very pretty pale lavender flowers.

H. UNDULATA

This species is well worth growing but it is its various varieties that are particularly valuable to the gardener. It is a medium-sized plant up to about 24 inches high. The very wavy leaves have a creamy-white center and broad margins of varying green. The flowers are a soft lilac. The popular variety albomarginata (also sometimes known as 'Thomas Hogg') has mid green leaves with irregular creamy-white margins. The variety erromena is a larger plant (up to about 20 inches in height) and has green leaves. H. u. univittata is another of the larger forms (up to about 18 inches high). The leaves are less wavy than the species and have a well-defined central area of creamy-white, with broad green margins. Finally, the typical form of H. undulata which is usually listed as H. undulata var. undulata (sometimes also known as variegata) has smaller, but wavy, leaves with an irregular central area of creamy white and narrow green margins. This plant typically grows up to about 10 inches in height and has lilac flowers.

H. VENTRICOSA

A tall species of hosta growing up to 24 inches in height with handsome mid green leaves. Its large flowers are violet-purple and of good substance. It has a very popular variety aureomaculata which has leaves with a bright sunshine yellow center and irregular deep green margins. The yellow central portion becomes much greener as the season progresses, making it look quite different by the time fall arrives.

H. VENUSTA

This plant is one of the smallest hostas in general cultivation, forming a mound only about 4 inches in height. Its small, pointed leaves are a mid green, each with 3–4 distinctive pairs of veins. The flowers are a rich violet blue. This is a good plant for a shady rock garden.

H. undulata univittata

HOSTA CULTIVARS

'Antioch' – A medium-sized hosta with whitish cream-margined leaves. Lavender-blue flowers. 14 inches high. Fast growing.

'August Moon' – A large hosta with pale gold leaves, at first opening pale green. Pale mauve flowers. Up to 24 inches high.

'Big Daddy' – A big hosta with very large round, puckered, blue leaves. White or pale blue flowers. Up to 36 inches high.

'Blue Moon' – A low, slow-growing hosta with round but tapering blue leaves. Mauve-blue flowers. Up to 6 inches high.

'Bressingham Blue' – A large hosta with rounded, puckered blue leaves. White flowers. Up to 20 inches high.

'Buckshaw Blue' – A medium-sized hosta with heart-shaped blue leaves with unusual upturned margins. It has very pale blue flowers. Up to about 14 inches high.

'Carol' – A medium-sized hosta with oval-shaped dark green leaves that have irregular white margins to them. The leaves have an attractive mealy bloom on them. It grows up to about 14 inches high.

'Chinese Sunrise' – A medium-sized hosta with glossy golden leaves with green margins. A spreading stoloniferous plant. Mauve flowers. Up to about 24 inches high.

'Elizabeth Campbell' – A large hosta with green-margined leaves, with creamy-white centers. Lavender flowers. Up to 24 inches high.

'Francee' – A large hosta with dark green leaves with attractive narrow white margins. Lavender flowers. Up to 24 inches high.

H. 'Krossa Regal'

'Frances Williams' – A very large and handsome hosta with puckered, deep bluish-green leaves, which are irregularly margined with a band of greenish-yellow. Very pale lavender flowers. Up to 32 inches.

'Ginko Craig' – A medium-sized hosta with narrowish leaves of a dark green with an irregular white margin. Purple flowers. Up to 14 inches. Very fast growing.

'Gold Edger' – A low-medium hosta that spreads rapidly to form good ground cover. Chartreuse green leaves. Lavender flowers. Up to 10 inches. Good for full sun.

'Gold Standard' – A very large hosta good for ground cover. Leaves are diffused chartreuse green and yellow turning to gold in sun but greener in shade. Pale lavender flowers. Up to 24 inches high.

'Golden Medallion' – A large hosta with puckered leaves that open yellow green but change to yellow. Near white flowers. Up to 18 inches high.

'Golden Prayers' – A medium-sized hosta with cupped, bright yellow leaves. Very pale lavender flowers. Up to 14 inches high.

'Golden Sunburst' – A large hosta with round leaves that start chartreuse and turn to yellow. Flowers white. Up to 20 inches high.

'Golden Tiara' – A small to medium-sized hosta with pale green leaves with yellow margins. Purple flowers. Up to 14 inches high.

'Ground Master' – A small to medium hosta with green leaves with an attractive undulating, white margin. Lavender flowers. Up to about 12 inches high. This is a good ground cover plant.

'Hadspen Blue' – A small to medium hosta with very good smooth, blue leaves. Lavender flowers. Up to 12 inches high.

'Halcyon' – A small to medium-sized hosta with excellent blue leaves. Violet flowers. Up to 12 inches high.

H. 'Halcyon'

'Honeybells' – A large hosta with undulating light green leaves. The fragrant, white flowers are tinged with mauve. Up to 24 inches. Increases rapidly.

'Hydon Sunset' – A very small hosta with small gold leaves, fading to green later in the season. Purple flowers. Up to 4 inches high.

'Krossa Regal' – A very large hosta with undulating pointed leaves of a glaucous blue. Flowers are a lavender pink. Up to 36 inches.

'Love Pat' – A large hosta with puckered deep blue leaves. Very pale lavender flowers. Up to 30 inches high. A good specimen plant.

'Midas Touch' – A medium to large hosta with puckered, round leaves that are a bright gold in color. It has pale lavender flowers. Up to 18 inches in height.

'Neat Splash' – A medium-sized hosta which has dark green leaves, splashed with gold, often more noticeable round the margins. Spreads by stolons. Lavender flowers. Up to 12 inches high.

'North Hills' – A large hosta with undulating, pointed dark green leaves with white margins. It is vigorously stoloniferous. Lavender flowers. Up to 20 inches. Good ground cover.

'Piedmont Gold' – A medium-sized hosta with heavily-veined golden leaves. White flowers. Up to 18 inches in height.

'Sagae' – A very large hosta with large, undulate, glaucous, frosted green leaves with cream margins. They are somewhat twisted. Very pale lavender, almost white, flowers. Up to 40 inches high. Makes a wonderful upright mound and is one of the best hostas. Also known as Hosta fluctuans 'Variegated'.

'Shade Fanfare' – A medium-sized hosta with light green leaves with cream margins. Lavender flowers. Up to 16 inches high.

'Snow Flakes' – A small hosta with narrow green leaves. The flowers are pure white, hence its name. Up to 8 inches high.

'Snowden' – A very large, spreading hosta with glaucous blue leaves. White flowers. Up to 34 inches high. Excellent specimen plant.

'Sum and Substance' – A very large hosta with chartreuse green leaves, almost gold in full sun. Lavender flowers. Up to 30 inches high. A very impressive hosta.

'Sun Power' – A large hosta with twisted leaves of a chartreuse to gold color. Lilac flowers. Up to 30 inches in height.

'Wide Brim' – A medium-sized hosta with bluish-green leaves with irregular cream margins. Pale lavender flowers. Up to 18 inches high.

'Zounds' – A large hosta with puckered, golden leaves. Pale lavender flowers. Up to 22 inches high.

Left: An all-green scheme with plain-leaved and variegated hostas adding color and form. Green flowers are provided by euphorbia at the back and *Helleborus argutifolius* in the center of the border.

BLUE LEAVES

'Big Daddy'
'Blue Moon'
'Bressingham Blue'
'Buckshaw Blue'
'Hadspen Blue'
'Halcyon'
'Love Pat'

GOLDEN LEAVES

'Gold Edger'
'Golden Medallion'
'Golden Prayers'
'Golden Sunburst'
'Piedmont Gold'
'Sum and Substance'
'Sun Power'
'Zounds'

GOLD MARGINS

H. fortunei
aureomarginata
'Frances Williams'
'Golden Tiara'
H. montana
'Aureomarginata'
H. tokudama
flavocircinalis

COLORED CENTERS

'Chinese Sunrise'
'Elizabeth Campbell'
H. fortunei albopicta
'Gold Standard'
H. undulata

WHITE OR CREAM MARGINS

'Antioch'

'Carol'

H. crispula

H. decorata

H. fortunei albomarginata

'Francee'

'Ginko Craig'

'Ground Master'

'Neat Splash'

'North Hills'

'Shade Fanfare'

H. sieboldii

H. undulata albomarginata

'Wide Brim'

SMALL LEAVES

'Golden Prayers'

'Hydon Sunset'

H. minor

H. venusta

BIG LEAVES

'Big Daddy'

'Bressingham Blue'

'Frances Williams'

'Krossa Regal'

H. montana

H. sieboldiana

'Snowden'

'Sum and Substance'

Left: A stunning foliage display in green, silver, blue and white. The hosta leaves contrast in form with the grass (*Phalaris arundinacea*) behind. White aquilegias provide interest with flowers.

107

OTHER SHADE-LOVING PLANTS

ACHLYS *(Vanilla Leaf)*

A genus of two perennial species of which A. triphylla is the most important. It is a native of the pacific coast of North America where it grows in damp, mountainous forests and woods and needs similar soil conditions in cultivation. Individual plants grow up to 20 inches high, but spread by rhizomes in the loose soil to form drifts. The flowers are cylindrical spikes of white stamens, without any petals, and appear in late spring to early summer, followed by reddish fruit. The foliage forms an attractive fan around the flower stalks.

ACTAEA *(Baneberry)*

A genus of eight perennial species. Several are in cultivation but two, A. alba (also known as A. pachypoda) and A. rubra, are the most commonly grown. From a gardening point of view the two species are quite similar except that the former has white berries and the latter red (the berries are poisonous). The plants are up to 36 inches, but taller by the time they are in fruit. The flower heads on both are clusters of white flowers that appear in late spring to early summer. The plant is grown more for the berries than the flowers. The divided foliage is very attractive. Increase by seed or division. Zones 4–9.

ALCHEMILLA MOLLIS *(Lady's Mantle)*

This is not a true woodland plant but will grow in light shade and is particularly useful for open shade such as on the north side of a building. The plant

Alchemilla mollis

grows up to 30 inches high, forming a dense clump of pleated, almost circular, leaves. The greenish yellow flowers appear on tall stems in airy sprays held above the foliage. The leaves and flowers are very attractive, the latter being fragrant. Useful in dry positions. Increase from seed. Zones 4–7.

ANEMONE *(Anemone)*

A genus of about 120 perennials of which a number will grow in shady conditions. The first of the year are the wood anemones, which include A. nemorosa with white flowers (zones 4–8), A. blanda (zones 4–8) and A. apennina (zones 6–9), both white, blue or pink, A. ranunculoides with yellow flowers (zones 4–8), A. trifoliata with white flowers (zones 6–8), A. sylvestris also with white flowers (zones 4–9), and several more. These are all low growing (up to 12 inches high) and spread underground to form medium to large colonies. Most flower before the leaves appear on

the trees. Another important group is the Japanese anemones including A. hupehensis and A. x hybrida (both zones 4–8). These are taller plants, up to 5 feet, that produce white or pink flowers in late summer and fall. These do not like such dense shade as the spring group but are perfect for dappled and, particularly, open shade as long as it is not too dry. Increase from division or root cuttings.

ANEMONELLA THALICTROIDES *(Rue Anemone)*

A delicate plant from eastern North America with which to carpet the woodland floor. It only grows some 8 inches in height and consists of thin wiry stems with pretty, divided leaves and wood anemone-like flowers in late spring and early summer. This is also a charming plant to grow under a shrub in a leafy soil or in a shady peat bed. Increase from seed or division. Zones 4–7.

Anemone hupehensis 'Hadspen Abundance'

Aquilegia vulgaris 'Nivea'

AQUILEGIA (Columbine, Granny's Bonnet)

A genus of some 70 species of perennials, grown mainly for their delicate flowers. Several species and many cultivars are grown in gardens but A. vulgaris is probably the most frequently seen and has been grown in gardens for centuries. It looks delightful in dappled shade but it is also a good plant for open shade. The plants grow up to 36 inches high. They flower in early summer in a wide range of colors of which shades of blue and pink are the most frequent. Like most woodland plants they prefer a moist soil but they will survive in much drier conditions. Many of the other species are worth trying. Increase from seed.

ARISAEMA

A genus of about 150 exotic-looking species. It is the hooded flower sheath (spathe) that is the attractive feature of these plants. They are often of smoky colors and delicately spotted. Many species are now grown in gardens where they need a rich moist soil and preferably a moist atmosphere. They are ideal for peat gardens as they can be quite difficult plants, but are best grown by more experienced gardeners to avoid disappointment. Increase from seed.

ARISTOLOCHIA
(Dutchman's Pipe)

A very large genus of some 300 species of which only a few are in cultivation. For the temperate shade garden the main one of interest is A. macrophylla. This deciduous climber can eventually reach 20 feet high. It produces curiously-shaped flowers that literally look like a smoker's pipe. This climber is ideal for a shady position but it can take two or more years before it establishes itself and begins to grow away. Increase from softwood cuttings. Zones 5–8.

ARUM
(Arum, Lords and Ladies)

A genus of 26 tuberous perennials of which only one or two are grown as shade plants. The most popular is A. italicum particularly in its form 'Marmoratum' (also known as 'Pictum'). This has a curious yellow flower spike enclosed in a pale green spathe (a hooded sheath) in early spring. However, it is the foliage for which this plant is grown. The dark green, arrow-shaped leaves are veined in silver. The leaves appear in early winter and continue through to late spring. It grows up to 12 inches high. Self sows from orange berries. Likes any shady position, preferably not too dry. Increase from seed or division. Zones 6–9.

ARUNCUS DIOICUS
(Goat's Beard)

This is a tall plant (up to 6 feet high), that is slowly spreading and likes to grow alongside woodland streams. The summer flowers are individually small but appear in a frothy mass of creamy white. The foliage is attractive and pinnate (with opposite leaflets). This plant will grow in dappled or open shade, but the soil should be moisture retentive (so incorporate plenty of leafmold). The form 'Kneifii' is shorter than the species (up to 36 inches high) and has very handsome, finely-cut foliage. Increase by division. Zones 3–7.

Arisaema japonica

ASARUM (Wild Ginger)

Several Asarum species are in cultivation, but there are just three that are relevant to this book. They all form low (up to 4 inches high), open drifts of heart-shaped leaves. Those of A. hartwegii, zones 6–8, are the most attractive with silver markings. They are mainly grown for their foliage as the flowers are hidden. The other two species are A. europaeum, zones 4–8, with rounded leaves and A. canadensis (Canadian wild ginger), zones 2–8. Its leaves are not as shiny and pretty as A. europaeum, but it is a lot less expensive. They grow well in woodland soils and are useful below trees and shrubs. Increase by division.

ASTILBE

A small genus of about 12 species but with many cultivars. These are a bit like the Aruncus except that the frothy flower heads come in a much larger range of colors, some of them quite lurid. They are some of the most colorful plants for shade, particularly open shade. They must have a moist soil or they will languish. The plants are up to 4 feet and flower in summer and fall. Increase by division.

ASTRANTIA (Masterwort)

A small genus of ten perennials of which A. major (zones 4–7), and its cultivars, and A. maxima (zones 5–8) are the most common. The flowers are tiny, contained in a ruff of bracts and resemble pin cushions. They are often green or greenish-white but there are pink and red forms. A. maxima is shell pink. Plants grow to 36 inches. Astrantia tolerates full sun, but prefers light shade and is perfect for open shade. Increase from seed or division.

AUCUBA (Spotted Laurel)

A genus of three evergreen shrubs of which A. japonica is the one most commonly seen. It has large glossy leaves, spotted or splashed in some cultivars. It will grow in quite dense shade and can be useful in a large garden. The yellow variegated varieties look like they are dappled with sunlight, and they brighten a dark corner. Deer enjoy feasting on aucuba. It can grow to 13 feet. Any reasonable soil. Increase by cuttings. Zones 6–10.

BERGENIA (Elephant's Ears)

These large-leaved perennials make excellent ground cover. They are generally leathery and glossy (B. ciliata is an exception with hairy leaves), often taking on reddish tones during winter. In spring, dense spikes of red, pink or white flowers stand out above the

Astrantia major 'Ruby Wedding'

Bergenia 'Silberlicht'

foliage (to 14 inches high). Grow in dappled, light or open shade. They do best in a moist leafy soil but will tolerate dry conditions. Increase from cuttings or division.

BETULA (Birch)

A genus of 60 deciduous trees and shrubs. These will not grow in shade but are useful for creating it. Those with small leaves produce the best dappled shade, but those, such as B. utilis jacquemontii (zones 5–7) that have white bark are probably the best to grow as they give all-year interest. They will grow in most soils. Propagate from seed.

BRUNNERA MACROPHYLLA

This perennial has hairy, heart-shaped leaves overtopped in spring by forget-me-not type flowers in blue. It is 18 inches high. There are a few cultivars. 'Hadspen Cream' and 'Dawson's White' are variegated foliage forms while 'Langtrees' has silver spots on the leaves. A white-flowered form is know as 'Betty Bowring'. Will grow in either light or open shade. The soil should have plenty of well-rotted organic material incorporated into it to keep it moist. Increase by division. Zones 3–7.

CALTHA PALUSTRIS
(Kingcup, Marsh Marigold)
This perennial has shiny foliage and large, bright gold, buttercup-like flowers in spring. It is a sprawling plant spreading from a central crown. Up to 24 inches high for large forms. It likes to grow beside or even in water, but can be planted in soil with a high moisture content. It looks best where it catches the sun, but will grow in dappled or open shade. There are several cultivars including several double and white forms. Increase by division or seed. Zones 3–7.

CAMELLIA
A genus of about 250 species (and innumerable hybrids and cultivars) of trees and shrubs. These plants are much loved for their beautiful white, pink or red flowers and glossy green leaves. They vary in size from small shrubs to large trees. In Southern California and other temperate parts of America (Pacific Northwest, the deep south and up through South Carolina) you can have camellias in bloom from November (the sasanquas) through to April or May if you plant many different varieties. Where winters are frosty, they bloom in fall or spring. Plant out of sight of the early morning sun, as this tends to thaw frosted buds too quickly, turning them brown. Plant amongst other trees and shrubs or in open shade, but not in a deeply shaded situation. Only plant in acid soils. Increase from cuttings.

Betula utilis jacquemontii

Campanula lactiflora 'Pouffe'

CAMPANULA *(Bellflower)*

A large genus of well-loved annuals and perennials, many of which will grow in light or open shade. Blue is the typical color of their bell-shaped flowers, but most species also have white forms and some have pink variants. Species that are worth growing in shady positions are C. lactiflora (zones 5–7), C. latifolia (zones 4–8) and C. latiloba (zones 4–8), all of which are tall plants. Also try low-growing ones such as C. poscharskyana (zones 4–7) and C. portenschlagiana (zones 4–7), both of which scramble up through shrubs. Grow in any good garden soil. Increase from seed or by division.

CARDAMINE

There are about 150 species in this genus. It is a valuable one as many species make very attractive shade-loving plants that flower in the spring. They nearly all tend to spread underground to form drifts of white, lilac or pink. None grows very tall, 10–12 inches being average, and they disappear below ground soon after seeding. They must have a moisture-retentive soil or they will peter out. Increase by division.

CARDIOCRINUM

A genus of three species of bulbs of which C. giganteum is the one most frequently seen. These are tall-growing (up to 10 feet) topped with a spike of large white, trumpet-shaped lilies. They are superb for growing amongst shrubs, particularly spring-flowering ones as these flower in summer. The bulbs take several years to reach maturity and die once they have flowered, but they usually provide offsets for the next generation. They need a very rich, moisture-retentive soil to produce their best. Increase by division or seed.

CAREX *(Sedge)*

A very large genus of plants of which a few will grow in shade. C. pendula (weeping sedge), zones 5–9, is a particularly graceful one to grow. It is clump forming with arching, swaying flower stems up to 5 feet tall. It self-sows and prefers moist conditions. Increase by division or seed.

CERCIS CANADENSIS *(Eastern Redbud, Judas Tree)*

This beautiful small tree grows on the fringes of woodlands or as an understory tree. In spring before the leaves open, it has bright pink, almost irredescent blossoms. Cercis occidentalis

Cardiocrinum giganteum

CHELIDONIUM MAJUS (Greater Celandine)

This plant has been grown as a herb for centuries, traditionally in a hedgerow, but it will grow in any form of shade. The type has small single yellow flowers in spring, but it is now generally grown in gardens in its more attractive double-flowered form. It grows to 36 inches. Increase from seed. Zones 5–8.

CIMICIFUGA (Bugbane)

A genus of 15 perennial species that are useful to the shade gardener, as not only are they attractive plants, but they flower in late summer to fall, when there is not much about. They are very upright plants, growing to 8 feet, with towering spikes of white or cream flowers. C. racemosa, black snakeroot (zones 3–8), and C. simplex, Autumn snakeroot (zones 4–8), are two of the best. The C. simplex Atropurpurea Group has beautiful dark purple foliage. They will grow in sun but are happier in light shade, particularly if the soil is moisture retentive. Increase by division.

CLEMATIS

A very large genus of climbing plants with many cultivars. These are popular and vary from species with small, delicately-colored flowers, to those where the flowers are great wheels of color. All like to have their roots in shade. The more subtle species look better in a woodland setting, but most can be induced to clamber up through trees. Some, such as 'Nelly Moser', prefer to be in shade or their color fades. Enrich the soil with organic matter and plant them 3 inches deeper than they were in their pots. Increase from cuttings.

(zones 7–10), is an excellent substitute for warmer parts of the country. These are important shade-tolerating trees. Increase by cuttings.

CHAENOMELES

A small genus of only three species of shrubs but one with many cultivars. Traditionally these are grown against walls, including shady ones, but they will grow as freestanding shrubs either in the open or under trees. They are untidy plants, unless pruned, but have brightly-colored flowers, often through winter into spring. These vary from white and pink through to red and orange. They produce attractive fruit later in the year. Increase from cuttings.

Colchicum autumnale 'Album'

CLINTONIA

A small genus of five species of wood-landers. They are all relatively short, up to 12 inches, and form large drifts on the woodland floor. In spring they carry small bell-shaped flowers, a bit like their close relations the lily-of-the-valley. C. uniflora (bride's bonnet) and C. umbellata have white bells, C. andrewsiana red-purple and C. borealis (bluebead lily) blue or white ones. They are perfect for growing under shrubs or along shady hedgerows. Increase by division. Zones 4–8.

COLCHICUM
(Autumn Crocus, Naked Ladies)

A genus of about 45 species of bulbs that superficially resemble crocuses, but are in fact not related to them. Most of the common species produce purplish flowers in fall, but there are white varieties. The flower stems are naked, the leaves not appearing until the following spring. Over time they will build up quite large colonies and are ideal for providing color toward the end of the year in a partial or open shade site.

CONVALLARIA MAJALIS
(Lily-of-the-Valley)

This must be one of the best loved of all woodland and shade plants. The arching stems, sometimes up to 12 inches high, carry delicately hanging white bells set off against the mid-green leaves that enclose the stems, creating a posy. These plants relish a leafy woodland soil and soon spread to create a fragrant carpet. Suitable for light or open shade. There are a number of cultivars, for example some with pink bells and others with

Convallaria majalis

Cornus canadensis

variegated leaves, but the typical species takes a lot of beating. Increase by division. Zones 2–7.

CORNUS (Dogwood)

A genus of about 45 species of shrubs and small trees, many of which like a woodland situation and grow in shade or open shade. One of the best is C. canadensis, bunchberry, (zones 2–7). This perennial creeps to create dense carpets. It grows to about 10 inches. Each stem carries a whorl of leaves topped by a white flower, which is, in fact, a number of white bracts. It makes good ground cover. There are many shrubby species that are worth trying. Cornus florida, zones 5–8, is a flowering dogwood native to the east coast of America. It is a lovely understory tree for woodland areas. Increase by division or cuttings.

CORYDALIS

A large genus of about 300 species and increasing as more are discovered, particularly in China. Many are tricky and need special treatment, but there are a number that are easy to grow in shady conditions as long as the soil is reasonably moist. Having said that C. lutea, zones 5–8, will grow in dry conditions including in shady walls. One of the best of recent introductions is C. flexuosa, zones 6–8, and its various cultivars. This has bright blue flowers. Except for climbing forms most corydalis do not grow much bigger than 12 inches or so. They will grow in any type of shady conditions, but they do particularly well on peat beds. Increase from seed.

CORYLOPSIS (Winter Hazel)

A genus of 30 deciduous shrubs, some of which flower in winter in light shade. Toward the end of winter, they produce fat, open catkins. They are lemon in color and fragrant. The bushes are very slow growing but can eventually reach 12 feet. The best ones are C. pauciflora, C. sinensis, and its various forms including veitchiana, (all zones 6–9) and C. spicata, zones 5–8. Increase from cuttings.

CORYLUS (Hazel)

A genus of 15 deciduous shrubs and small trees, the majority of which are in cultivation. They make good plants for creating shade, especially in a small garden. Two of them will not grow very tall (up to 20 feet, but can be kept lower by pruning) and yet will provide enough shade for a good-sized shade-bed. The flowers are produced in attractive, yellow catkins

Corylus avellana

from midwinter onwards. They can be coppiced to restrict their size and to produce wood for pea sticks and poles. C. avellana, zones 3–9 and C. maxima, zones 4–9, are the two most frequently seen of the corylus. Increase from cuttings.

CYCLAMEN

A bulbous genus of about 19 species. Not all are hardy but a few are and will grow in shade, often in dry shade. C. coum, zones 5–9, and C. hederifolium, zones 8–9, are two of the best. They respectively flower in midwinter and early fall. They are 4 inches high. The foliage makes an attractive ground cover until early the next summer. When happy they will quickly

self-sow and produce a carpet of plants after a few years. Plant under trees or shrubs, or in open shade. Increase from seed.

DAPHNE

A genus of about 50 small shrubs, many of which will grow in shade or open shade. For most shady positions D. mezereum (zones 5–8), with its purple flowers held tight to its stems, D. odora (zones 7–9), with its pinky-white flowers and D. laureola (zones 7–8), with its green flowers, are the best. These flower early in the year, often in winter. They grow to about 24 inches but some of the other species are larger. Most daphnes are worth growing for their scent as well as their appearance and D. mezereum is no exception. Plant in a good leafy soil. Increase from seed or cuttings.

DICENTRA (Bleeding Heart)

A small genus of 19 perennials and a few annuals. Although better known as part of the herbaceous border these plants, in fact, do better in light shade than they do in full sun. They are attractive both for their finely-cut foliage and for their arching stems of flowers, hanging like pendants. They mainly flower in early summer. One of the tallest is D. spectabilis (zones 3–9), which grows to 36 inches, though there is one climber, D. scandens (zones 6–8), that grows to four times this height, scrambling up through bushes. The many forms of D. formosa (zones 4–8), and C. eximia (zones 4–8) make excellent shade plants. All can be grown in light or open shade and do best in a moist, leafy soil. Increase by division.

Dicentra spectabilis

DIGITALIS (Foxglove)

A genus of 20 biennials or perennials, many of which are edge-of-woodland plants that can be grown in part or open shade. These all make tall spikes of flowers (up to 6 feet high), mainly in soft colors. The most commonly seen is D. purpurea (zones 4–8), with large purply-pink flowers. Although biennial, it self-sows prodigiously. Another good one is D. lutea (zones 3–9) with small yellow flowers, a short-lived perennial that also self-sows. There are plenty of others that are worth exploring. They will grow in any soil, but do best in richer mixtures. Increase from seed.

DICKSONIA (Man Fern, Tasmanian Tree Fern)

A genus of some 25 tree ferns, that will add a touch of exotica to any shade. The most frequently seen is D. antarctica which, given plenty of time (the life-span of several gardeners) and ideal conditions, will eventually reach 50 feet, but even at a young age will have very attractive fronds (leaves) that are 6 feet long, arching from a thick, hairy trunk. They like a moist soil and moist atmosphere. Increase from spores. Zones 9–10.

DISPORUM (Fairy Bells)

A small genus of woodland plants which are uncommon but worth getting to know. They are related to the Polygonatum and have nodding flowers hanging from upright stems. The colors vary but are generally white tinged with green or yellow. One of the most attractive and popular is D. sessile 'Variegatum' which has leaves striped with silver. This spreads underground to make a good ground cover.

119

Dryopteris filix-mas

EPIMEDIUM *(Barrenwort)*

A genus of about 25 perennial species. These are the doyen of perennial ground covers: they quickly cover the ground with handsome, heart-shaped foliage on thin wiry stems. Over the top of these extend further thin stems bearing dainty little flowers in an airy array. The flower color varies from white and yellow to reds and purples. Some are herbaceous and disappear underground for the winter, but others are evergreen. The latter need to be sheared over during late winter so that the new emerging foliage is not masked by the old, tired-looking leaves. Try one of the E. grandiflorum cultivars (bishop's hat, zones 5–8) as a first plant and then move on to explore the other species. The bigger species grow up to 14 inches high, but some of the smaller ones, such as the beautiful E. davidii (zones 5–9) are less than half of this. Best in a moist woodland-type soil, but they will tolerate a drier soil if necessary. Increase by division.

ERANTHIS HYEMALIS
(Winter Aconite)

This is a low tuberous plant that spreads to form large colonies when it is happy, growing to about 6 inches high. It only appears above ground between late winter and when the leaves on the trees start unfurling. The flowers are cheerful golden cups surrounded by neat ruffs of leaves. It does best in a leafy soil and can be planted under trees or shrubs or in open shade. Increase by division or from freshly-sown seed. A must for any shade gardener that can provide the right conditions. Zones 4–9.

This is only about 18 inches high or less, but other species, such as D. flavens, will grow to twice this. They need a moist leafy soil and light or open shade. Increase by division.

DRYOPTERIS *(Buckler Fern)*

A genus of about 50 species of ferns, many of which are worth growing either in the shade of shrubs and trees or in open shade to the north of a house or other wall. D. filix-mas (zones 4–8) is widespread in the wild and is likely to appear suddenly of its own accord in your shade bed, but it can, of course, be introduced there. It is not the most delicate fern but it is very attractive nonetheless. There are many different forms of buckler fern in cultivation, as there are also of D. affinis, the golden shield fern (zones 6–8). They prefer a moist woodland soil but will do well even in drier conditions. Increase from spore.

Eranthis hyemalis 'Guinea Gold'

EUCRYPHIA

A small genus of evergreen trees and shrubs for light shade. They are grown for their beautiful, fragrant flowers, pure white saucers with a golden central boss, appearing in late summer and fall; a valuable time. The leaves are leathery and can burn in severe frosts or winds. E. glutinosa (zones 8–10), E. x intermedia 'Rostrevor' (zones 9–10), E. milliganii and E. x nymansensis (both zones 8–9) are the most popular. With time they can all grow up to 30 feet. They grow best in acid soils, but will tolerate a little alkalinity. Increase from cuttings.

EUONYMUS (Spindles)

A large genus of shrubs and trees, many of which will grow in woodland or open shade. Many of the deciduous ones, such as E. europaeus (zones 4–7) are grown for their berries, while E. alatus, burning bush (zones 4–9), has winged stems that are attractive during the winter. There are also some evergreen forms of E. japonicus (zones 6–9) and E. fortunei, winter-creeper (zones 5–9), that have variegated foliage which shines out well in a shady position. The latter will climb through other shrubs or spread to form good ground cover. They do best in a rich moist soil, but they will also tolerate a certain amount of dry conditions. Increase from cuttings.

Fuchsia 'Thalia'

EUPHORBIA (Spurge)

This is an enormous genus covering all types of plants and all parts of the world. For the temperate woodland, there are a couple of stars and several other possibilities. The stars are two of the less spectacular spurges but they grow in woodland in the wild and one in particular will tolerate dry conditions. These are E. amygdaloides, the wood spurge (zones 6–9), and its subspecies E. a. robbiae. The latter is a very good plant for difficult positions in shade. There are many other spurges that grow in light or open shade. These include E. sikkimensis (zones 6–9), E. schillingii (zones 7–9) and E. griffithii (zones 4–9), especially its cultivars 'Fireglow' and 'Dixter'. Increase by division.

FUCHSIA

Fuchsias are associated with summer bedding but many prefer light shade to full sun. They are useful in borders or pots. Pots are better for tender varieties, which should not be planted out until after the frosts. Hardier species, such as F. magellanica (zones 6, with protection, to 10) can be grown outside all year in some areas, but are often cut back by frosts. They should recover. Increase from cuttings.

GALANTHUS (Snowdrops)

A genus of about 15 species of bulb, with many hybrids and cultivars. Few gardens can be without these delightful plants that light up shady places in the darkest months of the year. They can form large drifts in woodland or can simply be one or two clumps in a shady spot. By the end of spring, they disappear back underground. Plant and move the bulbs soon after flowering and split up the clumps every few years to prevent congestion. Any soil will do as long as it is neither too dry nor too rich. Increase by division.

GALIUM ODORATUM (Sweet Woodruff)

This will grow in deep shade and is great to put under mayapple (Podophyllum) because it provides ground cover when the mayapple disappears underground in late spring. It is a vigorous ground cover plant that survives poor soil and drought. Increase by seed or division. Zones 5–8.

GARRYA ELLIPTICA (Tassel Tree)

This shrub has the advantage that it will grow on a shady wall and it flowers from late winter onwards, when there is not much else to see. It can also be grown as a freestanding shrub, when it will eventually grow up to 16 feet. The flowers hang in silver-gray tassels. The evergreen leaves can be scorched by cold winds and hard frosts so protect it in exposed positions or extreme conditions. Will grow on any soil, although it does best in a fertile one. Increase from cuttings. Zones 8–10.

GAULTHERIA

A genus of about 170 species of evergreen shrubs, many of which will tolerate shade. They are grown as much for their decorative fruit as for their flowers. The fruits are spherical and often brightly colored, in shades of red, white and pink. They must have an acid soil, and it should be reasonably moist. Increase from cuttings.

Gaultheria procumbens

Geranium 'Patricia'

**GENTIANA ASCLEPIADEA
(Willow Gentian)**

This is a very large genus, but from the shade point of view there is only really one garden plant that is reliably happy with shady conditions and that is the willow gentian. This striking plant forms a mound of arching stems (up to 24 inches high) along the tops of which appear piercingly blue flowers of a typical gentian shape. Many other species tolerate a very light shade, but do need a bit of sun to do well. A rich, leafy soil is required. Increase from seed. Zones 6–9.

GERANIUM
(Hardy Cranesbill)

This genus of about 300 species and innumerable hybrids and cultivars is one most valuable to the woodland gardener. So many of them will tolerate light shade or at least the open shade provided by walls and fences. They vary in height from ground hugging to 30 inches or more. Some will scramble up through shrubs and other plants. Their flowers vary from pale pink through purple to blue. Some, such as G. macrorrhizum, make excellent ground cover, even for dry shade. It would take the rest of this book to list all that are suitable, so it is best to go to a reputable nursery and make your choice by sight. Increase from cuttings or by division.

GLAUCIDIUM PALMATUM

This perennial has beautiful flowers that are dish shaped and appear in spring. The plants are clump-forming and about 24 inches high. It is not the easiest of plants to grow but the effort is most rewarding. It needs a moisture-retentive soil and a cool, moist atmosphere. A peat bed is the perfect place. Increase from seed or by division. Zones 6–9.

HACQUETIA EPIPACTIS

This is a woodland plant that appears in midwinter. The flowers form small yellow mounds, but they are set off with a ruff of green bracts or leaves. Not a spectacular plant, but in winter it is most welcome. It only grows to 3 inches high. It will grow in any woodland soil where it will not be swamped by other plants. Increase from seed or careful division. Zones 5–7.

HAMMAMELIS
(Witch Hazel)

A small genus of 5 shrubs and small trees that are valuable for their winter flowering. The flowers are curious strap-like bundles of petals with an astringent fragrance, and which appear tight to the bare stems. The flowers are mainly yellow and gold, but H. x intermedia (zones 5–9), provides a range of orange and red forms. Any of the species are worth growing, but the many cultivars provide a better range of flowers. Witch hazels do not like alkaline soils. Increase from cuttings.

HEDERA (Ivy)

A genus of 11 climbing plants that can be used for climbing (on walls, fences and trees), trailing (in baskets and window boxes) or scrambling (as

Hacquetia epipactis

Hedera helix 'Chester'

ground cover). *H. helix, English ivy (zones 5–10), or one of its many cultivars, is a prime candidate but there are many others that will do the job. Those with bright variegated foliage will brighten up a dark corner. If used as ground cover, clip over every spring to keep it neat. Ivy will grow in any kind of soil. Increase from cuttings.*

HELLEBORUS (Hellebore)

A genus of 15 or so perennial species plus an increasing number of cultivars. These winter-flowering plants are becoming ever more popular. The clump-forming plants grow up to 18 inches high and carry dish-shaped flowers in a wide variety of colors from white, through green, pink and

purple to almost black. When out of flower the foliage is still an attractive feature for the rest of the year. All the species and many cultivars are in cultivation. They all like a light or open-shaded position with a well-drained but moisture-retentive soil. Increase from seed or division.

HELONIOPSIS ORIENTALIS

A rhizomatous perennial which forms a clump of strap-like leaves, from which, in spring, emerges a stem of nodding pink flowers. The plant grows up to 12 inches tall. Plant in light or open shade in a woodland-like soil. A peat bed is ideal. Increase by division. Zones 7–9.

HEMEROCALLIS (Day Lily)

This is a small genus of only 15 species but many cultivars. Day lilies are usually thought of in terms of sunny borders but they do very well in light or open shade. The plants form a slowly-extending clump of arching strap-like leaves above which tall leafless stems of flowers appear in summer. Each flower only lasts for a day, hence the name. The flower colors are mainly yellows and orange, but there are also shades of pink and mahogany. The plants grow up to 4 feet or more in height. They like a moist soil. There is a wide range of plants on offer and it is best to see them in flower before purchase. Increase day lilies by division.

HEPATICA

A small genus of 10 woodland plants that were once classified under Anemone. They are small plants, only up to 10 inches in height, but often much shorter. The bright blue, pink or white flowers appear in early spring above lobed leaves. The most common species are H. nobilis (zones 5–8), H. acutiloba (zones 4–8), H. americana (zones 3–8), and H. transsilvanica (zones 5–8). They all like a leafy woodland-like soil and light or open shade. They are ideal for a peat bed. They need humus-rich, well-draining soil to flourish. They also thrive in heavy, slightly alkaline soils. Increase from seed or division.

HEUCHERA (Coral Bells)

A genus of 55 perennials, several of which regularly appear in herbaceous borders. Although often grown in full sun, they prefer a bit of light shade and are ideal for open shade. They are grown both for their airy sprays of pink or greenish flowers and for their attractive leaves. Many modern forms have purple foliage, often with silver markings. However purple forms need more sun to retain their rich color. There are plenty of good plants from which to choose. Increase by division. Zones 4–8.

HOSTA

See pages 98–107.

HOUTTUYNIA CORDATA

This plant rapidly spreads through leafy soil to form a good ground cover. It is low plant but scrambles up through other plants, reaching up to 24 inches high. The flowers are small

domes of white, but the double form is also popular. The most popular form is 'Chameleon' which has heart-shaped leaves variegated with three colors. Plant in light or open shade. Increase by division. Zones 6–11.

HYACINTHOIDES
(Bluebell)

Bluebells are the star bulbs for shady positions. They can increase quickly to produce carpets of plants that only stay above ground during the spring. During this time they produce a haze of bright blue flowers. However they should be avoided in the small garden, as they do spread vigorously. Any good garden soil will suffice. Increase by division of the bulbs. Zones 4–9.

Heuchera micrantha diversifolia 'Palace Purple'

HYDRANGEA

Although often seen in full sun, many of these shrubs prefer a light shade, especially in hot areas. They are ideal for open shade provided by walls and fences, as long as the position is not too exposed. The most common is H.

Hemerocallis 'Mrs David Hall'

macrophylla (zones 6–10). Some, such as H. aspera (zones 6–9), are prone to late frosts and may need protection. H. anomala petiolaris (zones 4–9) is a climbing hydrangea that is perfect for a north-facing wall. Hydrangeas suffer from drought and should be given a moist, leafy soil. Increase from cuttings.

HYLOMECON JAPONICUM (Wood Poppy)

This belongs to the poppy family and has poppy-like, yellow flowers, the whole plant at a quick glance looking a bit like Welsh Poppy, Meconopsis cambrica. It grows up to 14 inches and spreads to form a small colony. As long as it has a reasonably moist soil it will grow in quite shady positions, more so than many other plants. It is also ideal for open shade. Increase by division. Zones 5–8.

IMPATIENS (Touch-me-not, Impatiens)

A very large genus of about 850 annuals and perennials of which only a few are of direct interest to the gardener. Some, such as the touch-me-not (I. noli-tangere), are grown as wild forms, while others such as I. walleriana, which is the standard impatiens used as a bedding plant in shady areas, have been very highly bred. The latter, although perennials, are generally treated as annual bedding as they are tender. They come in a variety of bright colors including red and orange and are useful for cheering up shady areas, especially when used in containers. They need a rich, moist soil or they will quickly wilt. Increase from seed or cuttings.

IRIS

This is a large genus of mainly sun-loving plants, but there are two species, Iris foetidissima (zones 7–9), and I. cristata (zones 4–8), that are woodlanders and grow well in light or open shade. I. foetidissima has glossy strap-like leaves that are evergreen, and pale bluish-purple flowers, sometimes tinged with yellow, in early summer. These are followed by bright red seeds that peep out of the split capsules, which are very attractive and often persist well into the winter. The plant grows up to 3 feet and is clump-forming. Does well on chalky soils, but will also grow in other conditions. I. cristata (crested iris) grows to 6 inches tall and spreads to make an excellent ground cover. In spring it produces sky blue or white blossoms. Tolerates dry shade. Increase from seed or division.

Iris foetidissima

JASMINUM NUDIFLORUM (Winter Jasmine)

Most jasmines are firmly wedded to the sun, but the winter jasmine, J. nudiflorum (zones 6–9), is useful for growing against a shady wall or fence. Its use is enhanced by the fact that its bright yellow flowers appear through winter. Although it is a shrub it can be trained to grow to some considerable height up a wall. It needs pruning to prevent it becoming a tangle of dead wood. Increase from cuttings.

JEFFERSONIA (Twin Leaf)

A small genus of two species of perennials. Both are well worth growing for their beautiful flowers that appear in late spring or early summer. They are not very big plants, only up to 8 inches high, but the simplicity of their flowers, especially the soft lilac blooms of J. dubbia (zones 5–7), makes them well worth growing. Their foliage is also an asset. They like a moist woodland soil and do best in a peat bed where they can be given attention as they may become swamped by neighboring plants. Increase from seed or careful division.

KERRIA JAPONICA

This shrub is most popular in its double form 'Pleniflora' although the simplicity of the single version has a lot going for it. There is also a variegated form with the leaves splashed with creamy-white. It is frequently planted in full sun, but it is quite happy in light or open shade. The bush will reach up to 10 feet but is often much less, especially 'Picta' which only grows to 36 inches. Any soil will do, even poor ones. Increase from cuttings. Zones 4–9.

KIRENGESHOMA PALMATA (Yellow Wax-bells)

This perennial is unusually beautiful. It grows up to 4 feet with a rhizomatous rootstock spreading to form small colonies. The stems are dark, almost black and the primrose yellow flowers are well set off against the maple-shaped leaves. It flowers in late summer or early fall. Plant in a woodland-type soil that does not dry out. Increase by division. Zones 5–8.

LAMIUM (Deadnettle)

A genus of about 50 species of perennials, several of which can be used in shade. They all have hooded flowers, but the color varies from red and purple through to white and yellow. The best for woodlands is L. galeobdolon, yellow archangel, with yellow flowers and silver-splashed leaves. It is a vigorous spreader. L. orvala forms round clumps and is much better behaved. This has large purple flowers and is useful for open shade. L. maculatum is another spreader but not so vigorous as yellow archangel. It has purple, white or pink flowers. They tolerate most soils but do best in a moisture-retentive one. Increase by division. Zones 4–8.

LATHYRUS VERNUS (Wild Peas)

This perennial grows in woodlands. It is a low plant, only 12 inches high, and, unlike most peas, it is not a climber but forms clumps. It carries small red-violet flowers in spring. There are also a few other color forms. It is a good plant for light or open shade and likes a woodland-type soil. Increase by division or from seed. Zones 5–9.

LILIUM (Lily)

A large genus of about 100 species, plus a lot of hybrids and cultivars. Although many lilies can be grown in full sun, a large number can be grown in light shade and are especially good for growing between shrubs. L. martagon, turkscap lily (zones 3–7), is particularly good for naturalizing under trees and shrubs. They require a soil that is free draining and yet moisture retentive, so add some grit to a leafy compost before planting them out. Increase from seed or division.

LIRIOPE (Lilyturf)

A genus of five species of evergreen perennials. The most commonly grown is L. muscari, big blue lilyturf (zones 6–10), and its cultivars. These grow in any situation from full sun to quite deep shade. They form tufts of grass-like leaves from which rise stems of mauve-blue flowers in the fall. They grow up to about 18 inches high. One of their big advantages is that as well as growing in deep shade, they will also tolerate dry conditions. Increase by division.

LONICERA (Honeysuckle)

A large genus of about 180 species of woody climbers and shrubs. Many of the climbers will start off in shade but will climb out into the sunlight. They are invaluable for creating shade over arbors and pergolas. The shrubs will grow among other shrubs but the one that will tolerate most shade is the low-growing L. pileata, zones 5–9. This

Lonicera periclymenum

is grown primarily for its mass of attractive small green leaves which create a very good ground cover. Increase from cuttings.

LUNARIA *(Honesty)*

A small genus of three species of which two are of possible interest to the shade gardener. L. annua *(zones 5–9),* in spite of its name is a biennial that will grow in shady positions. It reaches 4 feet or more with purple or white flowers in spring followed by large silver seed pods. The seeds themselves are visible through the transparent pods. L. rediviva *(zones 6–9),* is a perennial with light mauve or white flowers and smaller seed pods. The better the soil the better the plants in both cases, although L. annua will grow in poor conditions. Increase from seed.

MECONOPSIS
(Blue Poppy, Welsh Poppy)

This a medium-sized genus of about 45 annual and perennial species, most of which are in cultivation. They all like light shady conditions and will grow well in open shade. However, they all also like a moist atmosphere and are very difficult to grow in hot, dry areas. The easiest to grow is the yellow or orange Welsh poppy, M. cambrica *(zones 6–8).* This is a wonderful plant for quite deep shade, as its flowers appear to glow in the dark. Apart from the Welsh poppy all the others must have a rich soil that never dries out. Many of the species have vivid blue flowers, making them invaluable garden plants. Increase from seed.

Lunaria annua

Myosotis sylvatica

MERTENSIA VIRGINICA (Virginia Bluebells)

This pretty perennial grows well in light or open shade. It grows up to about 24 inches and has clusters of clear blue flowers that open from pink buds and are lightly fragrant. It needs rich, moist, woodland soil. It flowers early and disappears back under ground in late spring, so can be grown in dense shade under deciduous trees or shrubs. Increase from seed or division. Zones 3–7.

MILIUM EFFUSUM 'AUREUM' (Bowles' Golden Grass, Golden Wood Millet)

This plant is very valuable as grasses rarely grow well in shade. It is doubly valuable in that it is a light gold in color. This wonder plant grows up to about 18 inches with very light airy stems of flowers. It will grow in dry conditions but prefers something a little moister. When happy it will self-sow. A brilliant plant. Increase from seed or by division. Zones 6–9.

MYOSOTIS (Forget-me-not)

This is a genus of about 50 annual and perennial species, some of which will grow in light or open shade. The main garden-grown variety is M. sylvatica (zones 5–9) which is perfect for carpeting under shrubs or a shady wall as well as out in full sun. They self-sow and produce low carpets (12 inches high) of sky-blue flowers every spring. They also come in pink or white. They grow in poor conditions but prefer moist soil. Increase from seed.

OMPHALODES *(Navelwort)*

A small genus related to forget-me-nots, which also have blue flowers, occasionally white. The two that are mainly of interest to shade gardeners are O. cappadocica (zones 6–8), up to 9 inches high, and O. verna, creeping forget-me-not (zones 6–9), which is a good woodland plant. Both are creeping plants that will make an extensive ground cover when happy, which means a moist, leafy soil. They are excellent for both light and open shade. Increase by division.

OPHIOPOGON *(Lilyturf)*

A genus of four species of perennial that are increasing in popularity. They form creeping carpets of low tufts (6 inches high) of strap-like leaves and spikes of white flowers. Of most interest are O. japonicum and O. planiscapus. The latter has a form 'Nigrescens' which has black leaves making it very popular. They will grow in dry conditions but prefer moisture-retentive soil. Increase by division. Zones 7–10.

OXALIS ACETOSELLA
(Irish Shamrock)

A delightful plant with pale shamrock-like leaves and little white bells. It only grows to 4 inches but spreads to create small colonies. The plant appears, flowers and retires below ground in early spring. It must have woodland soil. Increase by division. Zones 3–8.

PACHYSANDRA TERMINALIS
(Japanese Spurge)

This perennial not only grows in quite dense shade, but also spreads to make perfect, glossy ground cover. It grows to about 8 inches and has highly glossy green leaves that seem to shine in the shade, lighting it up. The white flowers are small and relatively insignificant. Good woodland soil is needed to grow this at its best, but it will grow almost anywhere and seems to cope well once it becomes properly established. Increase by division. Zones 4–8.

PARIS *(syn. Daiswa)*

This is a genus of several perennial species. Most seem to do best in light or open shade although not many are in general cultivation. The two main ones are P. quadrifolia (zones 5–8) and P. polyphylla (syn. Daiswa polyphylla), zones 5–8. They both have curious flowers in that the petals have been reduced to golden threads which radiate out from a central black boss. They need to grow in a rich woodland-type soil. Increase by division or seed. Zones 5–8.

PENTAGLOTTIS SEMPERVIRENS
(Green Alkanet)

This plant is a bit rampant as it sows itself around rather freely but for those with space it makes a good ground cover. It grows up to 36 inches and has bristly leaves and bright blue forget-me-not flowers. It will grow in any type of soil, though humus-rich, damp soil is best, and grows in partial or deep shade. Increase from seed. Zones 6–9.

PERSICARIA *(Knotweed)*

A large genus of over 100 species. Some are absolute thugs and should not be allowed near a garden or you will not get rid of them. A few are 'safe' although most spread to some extent. P. affinis (zones 3–8) is a low-growing plant, up to 12 inches high, that forms a dense carpet of good foliage overtopped with spikes of pink turning to red and then brown. It is a

Persicaria affinis

valuable plant particularly for open shade but will also grow in light and dappled shade. Increase by division.

PHLOX

A genus of 67 perennial and annual species, of which a few are great for shade. P. adsurgens (zones 4–8), P. divaricata (zones 4–8), P. maculata (zones 5–8), and P. stolonifera (zones 4–8) are all good plants for such conditions. Each has a number of good cultivars, many with soft colors that shine out well in shade. They are low growing, up to about 12 inches high, and spread to make a small colony. They prefer moist, humus-rich soil, but will survive under more challenging conditions They can all be increased from cuttings or division.

PODOPHYLLUM
(Mayapple)

A small genus of 7 perennial species of which two grow in shade: P. hexandrum, Himalayan mayapple (zones 5–8) and P. peltatum, mayapple (zones 4–9). They are curious plants as the flowers appear above the unfolding leaves, only to duck under them and produce large plum-like fruit. The flowers are white or pink. They grow to about 18 inches high and spread out to form large clumps. They must have a moist, humus-rich soil. Increase from seed or division.

POLYGONATUM
(Solomon's Seal)

A genus of about 30 perennial species. These are wonderful plants for medium to open shade. Their gracefully arching stems grow up to 4 feet high and from them dangle nar-

row white or greenish white flowers in late spring. They build up colonies but never seem to be a nuisance. Increase by division. Zones 5–8.

POLYSTICHUM
(Holly Fern, Shield Fern)

A large genus of about 175 species of fern, many of which are suitable for the shade garden. P. setiferum, hedge fern (zones 6–9), is one of the best with a large number of cultivars. It grows up to 4 feet and is a beautiful fern, especially when unfurling. Propagate from division or spore.

PRIMULA (Primrose)

A large genus of over 400 species, plus many cultivars. Most species are in cultivation, but some are far too specialized for the general shade garden, although many will grow in a well maintained peat bed. Most flower in the spring. Fortunately, some of the commonest are still some of the best and most loved. P. vulgaris, common primrose (zones 4–8), is a good example. Polyanthus also grow well in dappled or open shade. Most of the candelabra primulas are easy to grow in light shade. They do need a moist soil (often doing best next to water) or they will languish and die out. Increase by division or from seed.

PULMONARIA (Lungwort)

The lungworts are a must for all shade gardeners. They have small, but bright, flowers from midwinter to spring and good foliage, often spotted or splashed with silver. They grow up to 12 inches high. Cut back the plants after flowering as they will produce a new set of leaves that will stay fresh

until the fall. They will grow in dry conditions but perform best in a moist, woodland-type soil. Increase the plants by division.

RHODODENDRON

A very large genus of about 800 species, plus hundreds of cultivars, of shrubs and trees that includes the azaleas. Nearly all the rhododendrons prefer shade and make ideal shrubs for the garden with their bright flowers and, in some cases, fragrance. They will only grow in areas with acid soils unless they are planted in containers of acid potting mixture. Increase from cuttings or by layering.

Rodgersia podophylla

RODGERSIA

A genus of six species of perennials, all of which are represented in the garden. These are quite large perennials, reaching up to 6 feet in good conditions. They are grown both for their decorative, architectural foliage and for their frothy plumes of creamy flowers that appear from midsummer onwards. They grow well in light or open shade, but they do need a moist, humus-rich soil. Propagate by division. Zones 5–8.

RUSCUS ACULEATUS
(Butcher's Broom)

Ruscus *is a small genus of six species of shrubs of which* R. aculeatus, *butcher's broom (zones 7–9), is grown in gardens because of its ability to cope with any shade, from quite deep to open, and for its bright red berries. It is evergreen with curious 'leaves' which are in fact flattened stems. The insignificant flowers, followed by the berries, appear in the center of the 'leaves'. It will grow in most soils including dry ones. Increase by division of its non-invasive suckers.*

SANGUINARIA
CANADENSIS (Bloodroot)

This enchanting plant is one of the delights of a woodland in spring. It has exquisite single white flowers, sometimes tinged with pink, that are sheathed like a posy in glaucous leaves. The double form is even more beautiful to many people's eyes, forming a ball of fine white petals. The plants only grow up to 6 inches and spread underground to form colonies. It must have a good woodland soil with plenty of leafmold. Increase by division. Zones 3–9.

SARCOCOCCA
(Christmas Box)

These shrubs are evergreen and make good ground cover. They will grow in most types of shade and will even survive in fairly dry conditions. Their flowers are insignificant to the eye but very prominent to the nose as they are extremely fragrant and will perfume the garden around them. They flower in midwinter, through to early spring. Most species only grow up to about 24 inches. Try S. confusa *or* S. hookeriana *(both zones 6–9). Increase by dividing their suckers.*

Ruscus aculeatus

SILENE (Campion)

A very large genus of about 500 species of annuals and perennials. Most are sun-lovers but a few, such as S. dioica, red campion (zones 6–9), will grow in dappled or open shade. This has dark pink flowers in spring and grows to 36 inches when suited. It will grow in most soils but does best in moister soils. Increase from seed.

SKIMMIA JAPONICA

This is a very important shade shrub with many cultivars. It is an evergreen with glossy leaves that shine out in the shade; it will grow up to 4 feet. It has white fragrant flowers in spring, followed by bright red berries that stay on through the winter. Both male and female plants are required to produce berries. It will cope with deep shade, but is better in open shade. It prefers an acid soil. Increase from cuttings. Zones 7–9.

SMILACINA RACEMOSA
(False Solomon's Seal)

This perennial produces large heads of creamy flowers in spring from arching stems 36 inches long. It expands to form a large clump. Another species sometimes grown is S. stellata which has smaller flower heads and spreads more rapidly to form large colonies. Both will grow in light or open shade. A moist humus-rich soil is needed. Increase by division. Zones 4–9.

SMYRNIUM PERFOLIATUM
(Perfoliate Alexanders)

A very attractive annual plant with bright yellow-green foliage and airy sprays of tiny golden flowers. In good conditions it reaches 4 feet or more. It

Sanguinaria canadensis 'Flore Pleno'

makes a very good plant for any shady position, except one in deep shade. It self-sows, but does not become a nuisance. Any soil will do, but it prefers a moist one. Increase from seed. Zones 6–10.

SORBUS (Mountain Ash)

A genus of about 100 trees and shrubs. Many of these do not grow to a great height, 15–20 feet at most, and therefore, like birch, make valuable trees for providing dappled shade in the average garden. Most are also attractive in spring with their flowers and then in fall with their handsome fruits and colorful fall foliage. They will grow on a wide range of soils. Increase from seed.

STYLOPHORUM DIPHYLLUM
(Celandine Poppy)

These perennials grow to 18 inches and have golden yellow, poppy-like flowers in summer, set off against a dull green foliage. Their flower color is good for illuminating shade. Plant in a moisture-retentive soil. Increase from seed if necessary, as it self-sows and grows well in heavy clay soil with little or no summer water. Zones 6–9.

SYMPHYTUM (Comfrey)

A genus of 35 species of perennials. These are not plants for the faint-hearted or those with a small garden, as they can spread very quickly. However they do form a very good dense

135

ground cover for shady areas and the large leaves make excellent compost. The tubular flowers come in blue, red, white or cream and appear in curious spirals among the foliage. Their height varies from quite low growing right up to 5 feet or more. They will grow in both light or open shade. Plant in any type of soil, but a humus-rich one is preferred. Increase comfrey by division or root cuttings.

TELLIMA GRANDIFLORA (Fringe Cups)

This is a very attractive plant for shady areas. It flowers in the spring on arching stems up to 24 inches high which are carried above the clump of foliage. The flowers are small but carried in quantity along the stems, their color being white, tipped with red. They give an airy appearance. They will grow in most soils but are not happy if it is too dry. Increase from seed, but self-sown seedlings are usually provided. Zones 4–8.

TIARELLA (Foam Flower)

A small genus of five species of perennials. They are spreading plants that quickly form quite large colonies but rarely become a real nuisance. T. cordifolia (zones 5–9), and the similar T. wherryi (zones 5–9), are the two most commonly-grown species. They are grown both for their attractive foliage and for the haze of flowers that hang above it during the summer months. The flowers are white tinged with pink. They are low growing, not reaching much above 12 inches in height. They are not sun lovers and grow well in medium to open shade. Increase by division.

TOLMIEA MENZIESII (Piggyback Plant)

This is a spreading plant which, until recently, was better known as a house plant. Its ivy-shaped leaves form a good ground cover for a shady site. Above them on arching stems hang tiny green bells in late spring. There is

a good variegated form known as 'Taff's Gold' that is especially useful for lightening up a dark corner. It grows to 30 inches or so. The piggyback plant prefers cool, moist conditions. Increase by division or from seed. Zones 6–9.

TRILLIUM (Wake Robin, Trillium)

Trilliums are a must for any woodland gardener as long as they can be provided with a moist, leafy soil and the right weather conditions. They will grow in any shade, from medium to open. It is the white-flowered wake robin, Trillium grandiflorum (zones 5–8), and its double form 'Flore Pleno', that are the most popular but there are many more to explore including the fragrant T. luteum, the yellow trillium (zones 5–8). Grow somewhere where they can be readily appreciated. These are good subjects for a peat bed. Increase is by careful division or from seed.

TRICYRTIS (Toad Lily)

A genus of some 16 or so perennial species, several of which are regularly grown in shady gardens. They are grown for their intriguing, upward-facing flowers which are available in a range of rich, muted colors. They have a pale base color to the petals and are then strongly marked with purple or red spots. They appear from late summer well into fall, a valuable time for shade-loving plants. The height varies but some reach 4 feet. They need to have a moist woodland-type soil and can be planted in any conditions from light to open shade. Increase by division.

Vinca difformis

Viola odorata

UVULARIA
(Bellwort, Merrybells)

These enchanting plants are related to the Solomon's seal, although their stems are generally upright rather than arched. They spread underground to create small colonies, but do not usually become a nuisance. Their flowers look like limp pieces of yellow rag and are rather attractive, in a funny way, although not at long range when they would be hard to see. Bellworts grow up to 30 inches in height and must have a moist, humus-rich soil to do well. Good subjects for a peat bed. Increase by division.

VANCOUVERIA

This is a small genus of three perennial species that are closely related, and look similar to, the epimediums. They are creeping plants that form dense colonies of attractive ground cover foliage up to about 12 inches high. The white or yellow flowers appear in spring and resemble dancing stars held above the handsome foliage on thin wiry stems. Any of the three species are well worth growing

in the shade garden. They do best in a moist, leafy soil, but will survive in drier conditions. Increase by division.

VINCA (Periwinkle)

A genus of six species of shrubby plants. They flower better in full sun, but they will grow well in shade, often dense shade. The commonest is V. minor, lesser periwinkle (zones 4–9), and its various cultivars. This flowers in the spring, but V. difformis (zones 8–9), has the valuable attribute of producing its very pale blue or white flowers for longer. It forms taller clumps than V. minor, reaching 18 inches or higher if allowed to scramble through shrubs. They will grow on most soils. Increase by division.

VIOLA (Viola, Violet)

A genus of 500 annual and perennial species and their numerous cultivars. Many are sun lovers but most of the forms commonly grown in gardens prefer to be provided with at least a bit of shade. They come in a wide range of flower sizes and colors and are particularly useful for beds in open shade. Pansies (Viola x wittrockiana) are good for shady containers. In woodland areas, sweet violets, V. odorata (zones 7–9), which come in deep purple and also a white form (V. o. 'Alba'), and several other species are a better choice. They all prefer a soil that does not dry out too much. Many spread to form soft mounds, while others form large and rather thuggish colonies. Many self-sow. Violas can be increased by cuttings or seed. Zones 4–10.

WALDSTEINIA TERNATA

This perennial is commonly grown in gardens. It is a low-growing plant, up to about 8 inches high, that spreads to form mats of good ground cover. In early summer the foliage is lit up by masses of yellow flowers. It must have a moist woodland-type soil and will grow in conditions from medium to open shade. Increase by division. Zones 3–8.

Waldsteinia ternata

HOSTA SUPPLIERS

√ Humber Nurseries
RR#8
Brampton, ON
Canada
L6T 3Y7

√ Mason Hogue Gardens
RR#4, 3520 Durham Road#1
Uxbridge, ON
Canada
L9P 1R8

Holes Greenhouses and Gardens
101 Bellrose Drive
St. Albert, AB
Canada
T8N 8N8

Rainforest Gardens
13139 224th Street
Maple Ridge, BC
Canada
V4R 2P6

Marvelous Gardens
8929 1st Street
Surrey, BC
Canada
V4N 3N5

√ Stirling Gardens
RR#1 Morpeth
Ontario
Canada
NOP 1XO

The Hosta Garden
47 Birch Grove
London W3 9SP
United Kingdom

Anne and Roger Bowden
Cleave House
Sticklepath, Okehampton
Devon
EX32 2NN
United Kingdom

Apple Court
Hordle Lane, Lymington
Hampshire
SO41 0HU
United Kingdom

Beth Chatto Gardens
Elmstead Market
Colchester, Essex
CO7 7DB
United Kingdom

Goldbrook Plants
Hoxne, Eye
Suffolk
IP21 5AN
United Kingdom

Marchants Hardy Plants
(Graham Gough)
Marchants Cottages, Ripe Road
Laughton
East Sussex
BN8 6AJ
United Kingdom

Merriments Gardens
Hawkhurst Road
Hurst Green
East Sussex
TN19 7RA
United Kingdom

Micklefield Market Garden
The Poplars
Micklefield
Stowmarket
Suffolk
IP14 5LH
United Kingdom

Banyai Hostas
11 Gates Circle
Hockessin
Delaware 19707
USA

Schmid Gardens
5809 Westwood Blvd
Jackson
Michigan 49203
USA

Walden-West Hosta
5744 Crooked Finger Road
Scotts Mills
Oregon 97375
USA

Coen Jansen
Vaste Planten
Konigsvaren 35
7721 HM Dalfsen
Holland

Gotemba Nursery
59 Nagatsuke
Gotemba-shi
Shizuoka 412
Japan

SOCIETIES

American Hosta Society
c/o Robyn Duback
2802 NE 63rd Street
Vancouver
Washington 98662
USA

British Hosta and
   Hemerocallis Society
Linda Hinton
Toft Monks
The Hithe
Rodborough Common
Stroud
Gloucestershire
GL5 5BN
United Kingdom

Hardy Plant Society
c/o Pam Adams
Little Orchard
Great Comberton
Worcestershire
WR10 3DP
United Kingdom

Netherlands
   Hosta Society
Arie Van Vliet
Zuidkade
97 2771 DS
Boskoop
Holland

Left: Hosta fortunei
aureomarginata
nestles under a Japanese
maple, *Acer palmatum
atropurpureum.*

Index

Acknowledgments

The publishers would like to thank the individuals who supplied the photographs on the following pages:

Clive Nichols Garden Pictures: Back jacket inset; 1; 6 (Turn End Garden, Bucks.); 8 (designed by Jill Billington); 11 (Longacre, Kent); 13 top right; 16; 19; 20 (Beth Chatto Garden, Essex); 21 bottom; 23; 25 top left and top right; 26 left; 27 left; 28; 30 right (White Windows, Hampshire); 32; 33 left and right; 35 top left and bottom; 40 top; 42 (designed by Olivia Clarke); 44; 46 top left (designed by Jill Billington); 47 (Vale End, Surrey); 48; 52 (Greystone Cottage, Oxon); 53 bottom right; 60 top (designed by XA Tollemache); 62 and 63 (designed by Myles Challis); 64; 65 top left and top right; 66 top; 67 bottom; 68 top (Chenies Manor, Bucks.); 69 left (designed by Ann Frith); 69 right; 70; 71 top right; 72; 73 bottom left and right; 74 (Benington Lordship, Herts.); 75 left (designed by Jane Nichols); 75 right; 77 top; 78 (Longacre, Kent); 80 top (Mrs Glaisher, Kent); 81 left (Savill Gardens, Berks.); 83 left and right; 85 bottom; 88 top; 92 (Chenies Manor, Bucks.); 93 top right; 94 (designed by Wendy Lauderdale); 98 left; 100 top; 101; 106 (designed by Elisabeth Woodhouse); 109; 110; 121; 122; 128; 130; 131; 134

John Glover Photography: Front jacket; main back jacket; 12; 13 bottom; 14 left and right; 18; 21 top; 24; 34; 35 top right; 36 bottom; 38 top; 39; 41 bottom; 49 top right and bottom; 51; 56 right; 57 bottom; 61 top; 68 bottom; 77 bottom; 82; 85 top left and top right; 86 bottom; 87 left; 89 top; 93 top left and bottom; 95 top and bottom; 97; 98 right; 99 left; 100 bottom; 103; 104; 111; 112 bottom; 113; 115; 116; 117 top and bottom; 118; 119; 120; 123; 125; 126; 133; 135; 137 top and bottom; 139

Catriona Tudor Erler: 17 top; 61 bottom; 76; 79 top

Graham Strong (Clive Nichols Garden Pictures): 71 top left; 79 bottom

Paddy Wales: 53 bottom left

All other photographs taken by Neil Sutherland, © Quadrillion Publishing Limited.

The publishers would also like to thank:

Merriments Gardens, Hurst Green, East Sussex for allowing us to take the following pictures in their garden: 17 bottom; 96 left
Murrell's Plant & Garden Centre, Pulborough, West Sussex for the loan of plants for photography.